THE HISTORY OF

ENGLISH INTERIORS

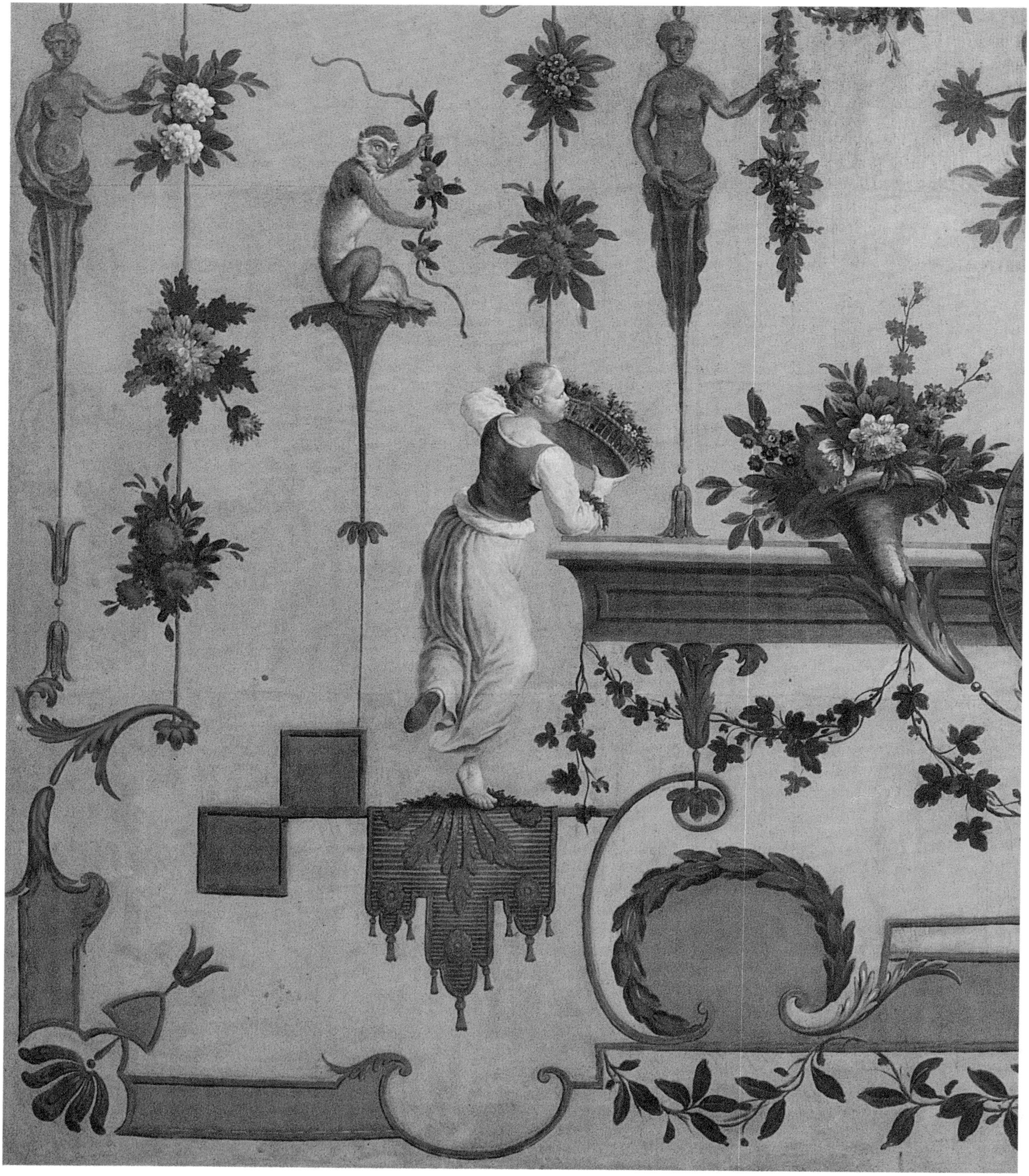

ENGLISH INTERIORS

An Illustrated History

Alan and Ann Gore

PRINCIPAL PHOTOGRAPHS BY
PETER APRAHAMIAN

Thames and Hudson

To J.B.F.

and to Edward Hudson, the founder of *Country Life*,
and all the succeeding generations of contributors who,
week after week, for nearly a century have shed so much
light on the domestic architecture and decoration
of this country

First published in the United States in 1991 by
Thames and Hudson Inc., 500 Fifth Avenue,
New York, New York 10110

Library of Congress Catalog Card Number: 90-70056

Design by James Campus

Printed and bound in Great Britain

FRONT ILLUSTRATIONS

Endpapers: detail of the painted panelling in the Bower, Castle Ashby, *c.*1630.

Page 1: «Frederick Elegantly Furnishing a Large House», satirical print, *c.*1782.

Frontispiece: detail of «grotesque» painting, by Andien de Clermont, on the ceiling of the hall at Wentworth Castle, *c.*1745.

ACKNOWLEDGEMENTS

21 Reproduced by gracious permission of Her Majesty the Queen; 3, 4, 9, 12, 18, 19, 23, 28, 29, 32, 49, 51, 52, 53, 54, 56, 57, 59, 63, 72, 73, 75, 78, 79, 81, 82, 83, 86, 89, 90, 91, 92, 111, 117, 132, 133, 141, 142, 145, 146, 148, 155, 156, 157, 158, 162, 163, 164, 165, 166, 168, 170, 176, 182, 185, 189, 199, endpapers, Peter Aprahamian; 7, 47, 116, John Bethell; 10, 15, 58, 71, 85, 93, 98, 108, 134, 154, 181, 187, 188, 190, 191, 193 Bridgeman Art Library; 43, 149 © British Architectural Library/RIBA; 125, 159, 179, 183, 184, 196, 201 Christie's; 14, 45, 49, 50, 70, 77, 95, 106, 113, 115, 128, 131, 139, 140, 147, 153, 198, 200, 203, 209 *Country Life*; 41 Photo: Courtauld Institute of Art; 212 Photography by Anthony Denney, kind permission of House and Gardens; 41, 47 Devonshire Collection, Chatsworth, reproduced by permission of the Chatsworth Settlement Trustees; 31 English Heritage; 120, 126, 138 Angelo Hornak; 190 Oscar and Peter Johnson Ltd., London; 169 Keele University, Staffs; 13, 16, 22, 26, 44, 48, 65, 69, 150, 192 A.F. Kersting, London; 30 Kirklees Museum Services; 42 Courtesy The Master and Fellows, Magdalene College, Cambridge; 58 Mallet and Son (Antiques) Ltd., London; 202, 204, 205, 206, 210 Millar and Harris London; 211 Derry Moore Photography Ltd., London; 27, 39, 46, 74, 96, 102, 105, 112, 136, 152 National Trust Photographic Library; 99 Royal Academy; 64 Scala, Florence; 103, 104 By Courtesy of the Trustees of Sir John Soane's Museum; 8 Society of Antiquaries of London; 24, 124, 160 Sotheby's; 110 Toledo Museum of Art, Ohio. Gift of an Anonymous Donor; 20, 25, 35, 36, 38, 40, 60, 62, 66, 67, 68, 80, 85, 87, 88, 100, 114, 122, 130, 135, 151, 161, 167, 171, 178, 180, 193 Courtesy of the Board of Trustees of the Victoria and Albert Museum; Half-title, 61, 94, 97, 118, 119 The Lewis Walpole Library, Yale University; 177 Weidenfeld and Nicolson; 187, 191 Christopher Wood Gallery, London; 33, 34, 144 *The World of Interiors*.

The location of some interiors is not stated in the captions; this is at the request of the owners.

CONTENTS

PREFACE

In compressing the history of decoration in English houses from 1066 to 1966 into one volume it is only possible to cover the subject in the broadest of terms. Happily, the scholarship devoted to the subject, especially since World War II, has underpinned and promoted a much greater interest, with the result that a number of books have and are being published covering specific periods and styles as well as studies of various aspects of decoration such as textiles. Our aim in this present book has been to provide a general background, laying particular emphasis on the, often frequent, recurrence of various themes and details of decoration, as well as placing the many revivals of past styles in their historical context.

We have tried, wherever feasible, to illustrate the many aspects of decoration from examples in smaller houses rather than in their grand and palatial counterparts. This has only been made possible through the skill and patience of Peter Aprahamian, who took the specially commissioned photographs and to whom we are very grateful. We would also like to thank Julia Brown for beavering away tirelessly to find most of the other illustrations, and Mrs Costello at the *Country Life* library who has solved many problems, often last-minute ones, with unruffled efficiency.

We are much indebted to all those who have allowed us to photograph in their houses. In particular Miss Jane Kimber, Commander and Mrs Woolner, the Marquess of Northampton, Sir Edmund Fairfax-Lucy, Mr Lionel Stopford Sackville, Mr James Hervey-Bathurst, Commander Andrew Fountaine, Mr and Mrs Geoffrey Holbech, Sir John and Lady Wiggin, Mrs Fyfe-Jamieson, Mr James More-Molyneux, Mr Rupert Galliers-Pratt, Lord and Lady St. Oswald, Mr and Mrs Brian Stein, Sir John and Lady Molesworth-St. Aubyn, Mrs Borno and Mr R.H. Fryer, Principal of Wentworth College. We would like to thank them and many others for their patience and kindness as well as Mr William Craven, Major Michael Pickard and other officials of the National Trust. Our special thanks to Anthony Wells-Cole for his generous help at Temple Newsam.

3. Detail of the upholstery of the State bed at Drayton, *c.*1701

INTRODUCTION

The challenge of a bare wall seems to have stimulated man's creativity from earliest times. Archaeology and historical and scientific research have furnished a number of clues to the early embellishment of houses in Britain. What emerges from such research is the certainty that there was considerably more decoration than was once thought, but the gaps in our knowledge are likely to remain vast. An excavated Roman mosaic floor may establish one feature and through Mediterranean precedents we can conjure up a Roman house, but we shall never know the level of sophistication that was achieved in wall paintings or furnishing in this provincial outpost of the Empire. No amount of imagination can summon up a vision of how rooms were decorated between the departure of the Romans and the arrival of the Normans in 1066. The recorded fact that Saxons used wall cloths is hardly of great interest but discoveries of highly ornamented jewellery lead one to think that such craftsmanship cannot have been confined to personal adornment.

The existence of Norman and early medieval buildings, however mutilated, places one on marginally surer ground, especially when a new discovery throws light on some aspect of decoration – such as the uncovering, in 1945, of the earliest known secular wall painting [pl. 4]. The fragile nature of such decoration and the infinitely more ephemeral quality of textiles inevitably leave whole areas out of reach except for the evidence found in illuminated manuscripts. Colour, too, is likely to remain largely a matter of conjecture – colour fades and perceptions vary, often alarmingly, from one person to the next, rendering descriptions inexact and sometimes confusing.

What we can be certain of is the persistent desire to evoke the past. The romance of the past is not the prerogative of the Romantic Movement of the late eighteenth and early nineteenth century – even the Romans looked back to the golden age of Greece. Revivals of one kind or another are seemingly an essential ingredient of decoration. Men and women in jeans sitting in a 'Georgian' room appear neither illogical nor incongruous to our eyes while the idea of Sir Samuel Rush Meyrick planning to dress up the villagers in medieval costume to match his medieval house, newly built around 1830, seems to us absurdly eccentric.

The English may be particularly adept at stealing from the past but they have also plundered Italy and France for ideas – a few month's truce in the middle of the Napoleonic Wars and the English were in Paris to search out the latest fashions in which to drape their rooms – and themselves. The influence of the past and the influence of Continental ideas are recurrent themes in the history of English decoration.

4. The paintings at Longthorpe Tower date from the 1330s and every wall of this small square room on the first floor is elaborately decorated with religious or secular stories and themes interspersed with birds and animals. Red and yellow ochres are the predominant colours with vermilion, greys and creams now faded but originally very rich.

I

GALLIC INFLUENCE AND GOTHIC ASCENDANCY

The influence of the French on the decorative arts in England has been a constantly recurring theme in the history of decoration. For four hundred years, from the Norman Conquest in 1066 until the end of the Hundred Years War in 1453, this influence was at its most dominant and pervasive. The ties between the two countries during this period were so inextricably interwoven that decorative schemes and details were virtually identical, even if the English versions were sometimes a trifle provincial.

For many of these four hundred years the Church led the way in most aspects of decoration. The Church was both inviolate and rich throughout a period when civil strife was frequent. The variations between the decoration of ecclesiastical and secular buildings occurred almost always as a result of the quest for comfort, for instance in the use of hangings and wainscoting for insulation purposes. Even in the embellishment of fireplaces the motifs and mouldings derived from the architectural decoration of churches.

The development of style was a slow process from the massive columns and rounded arches of the Romanesque of the Normans to the final flowering of the Gothic with its huge areas of windows. The architectural decoration of the Norman castles was confined to the use of mouldings around the arches that formed the windows, doorways and fireplaces. Shafts capped by an often crude form of cushion or scalloped capital reached to the springing of the arch, where the moulding round the arch itself was often carved in a chevron pattern [pl. 7].

Defence and weather dictated the small size of the windows in Norman castles and fortified manors. With the introduction of the Gothic pointed arch towards the end of the twelfth century, and more settled conditions, the long progress towards larger windows began. At first a circular or quatrefoil window was introduced above the central mullion or column that separated two narrow windows [pl. 15]; from this, tracery developed becoming ever more elaborate – ogee and trefoil mouldings proliferated to form beautifully carved and intricate patterns. By the fifteenth century stained glass added one more decorative element that had formerly been confined to churches [pl. 5].

Glass was extremely expensive throughout the period and windows were divided horizontally by a mullion, the lower division often with iron bars and shutters and the upper glazed with small panes in a movable frame. The movable glass would be packed up for safety when the owner was absent. By the middle of the fifteenth century it was more readily available and windows became larger and fixed. Stone seats set on either side of deep window embrasures first appear in late Norman times, providing some seclusion from the main body of the hall. These areas were used for sewing or playing games. They had

5. Six of sixteen armorial stained glass windows, *c.*1465, with the arms of Henry VI and his wife demonstrating the Lancastrian loyalties of the owner of the manor house. The remaining lights, each about 18 × 36 inches (45 × 90 cm), show the arms of neighbouring families and the owner's own motto 'Feythfully Serve'.

6. Christine de Pisan presenting her book to Isabel of Bavaria, who married Charles VI in 1385. The arms of France and Bavaria alternate on the hangings and the bed curtains are 'bagged'. Only the upper windows have glass but the lower removable shutters are also glazed. (British Library, London.)

7. The great chamber at Castle Hedingham, *c.*1130. Originally the walls would almost certainly have been painted and later covered with tapestry or hangings. The Norman arch and incised chevron patterns found favour again in the early nineteenth century (see pl. 152).

the advantage of good light and could be warmed with a portable brazier. The window embrasure soon expanded into the bay, or oriel, window. Any form of seclusion was obviously desirable when the entire household, including servants, had to eat, sleep and live in the hall. But such rudimentary attempts at privacy were unlikely to be tolerated if the owner could afford a private room for himself and his family. The solar or great chamber provided this desirable accommodation and early examples of this new room exist from the second half of the twelfth century.

Despite further additions throughout the medieval period, such as lodgings for guests, the hall retained its importance as the room of reception until the middle of the sixteenth century and as such it remained the place for conspicuous display and decoration. The discomfort caused by fires laid on the floor in the centre of the great hall led inevitably to the wall fireplace. The Normans had used them on the first floor of castles, where a central hearth would, in any case, have been impractical but, by the end of the twelfth century a hood over the fireplace provided even more protection against smoke-filled rooms [pls 10, 26]. Whether hooded or not, the fireplace, then as now the focal point of a room, became an obvious feature for embellishment and reflected the various changes of decorative style. In the grander houses they were often very elaborately carved and sometimes suitably emblazoned with heraldic devices.

It is sad that in their restoration of medieval buildings the Victorians were under the misapprehension that our forebears favoured bare stone walls, incidentally removing valuable evidence of early decoration. It is clear that the value of insulating the walls was fully appreciated by the builders of medieval houses. Plaster of Paris succeeded simple whitewash on stone walls, providing some insulation. These surfaces were then decorated, often with red painted lines to imitate stonework but sometimes more elaborately as at the Tower of London in 1238, when Henry III ordered, for Queen Eleanor, 'the walls of the queen's chamber, which is within our chamber . . . to be whitewashed and pointed, and within those pointings to be painted with flowers'. Even more elaborately in 1240 'the chamber of our queen in the aforesaid Tower [is to] be wainscoted without delay, and to be thoroughly whitened internally, and newly painted with roses.' Wainscot seems to have been the most usual method of insulating rooms – tapestry was not introduced into England until the fourteenth century – and fir, being easily worked, was imported from Norway for this purpose. This wainscoting was quite simple and consisted

8. A copy of one of the late-thirteenth-century murals painted for Henry III but destroyed in the fire at the Palace of Westminster in 1834. 'Tranquility' stands on 'Anger' holding a switch and a shield painted with the leopards of England.

of narrow vertical boards joined together with butt joints or, more usually, a simple form of tongue and groove. It was generally painted, certainly in the more important rooms. We know from the accounts of Henry III that green was his favourite colour for decoration, and green and gold or even silver are often combined, as at Winchester Castle where the king's Painted Chamber was to have wainscot 'painted with green colour' and the queen's wardrobe was to have 'green paint and golden stars'. There are a number of beguiling contemporary references to the wall decoration being 'spangled' or 'scintillated' with gold. At Winchester Castle he also ordered green starred with gold as the background for paintings of 'histories' from the Old and New Testaments in circles on the wainscot.

The monochrome appearance of the interior of surviving early medieval castles bears very little relationship to what they looked like originally. In addition to the painted wainscot and to the linear decoration of plaster walls there were also representational paintings, as in the famous Painted Chamber in the Palace of Westminster, destroyed by fire in 1834. Very fortunately these had been copied in 1819 [pl. 8] and provide evidence of the decoration of a king's chamber. Henry III used this room as a bedroom and audience chamber and decorated it with a large mural of the Coronation of Edward the Confessor. The virtues of Largesce (generosity) and Debonerete (tranquillity) faced each other on the splays of the window opposite the royal bed. The first record of an English state bed is from this period and was from this palace. It had green posts powdered with gold stars and was painted by one Master William for a fee of twenty marks. In this chamber there was also an extensive series of Old Testament stories ranged round the room but these were probably executed some time in the 1290s for Edward I and Eleanor of Castile. In royal palaces and the dwellings of the rich, colours would have been brilliant and gold was employed fairly freely, as we have seen, but wall painting was also used as decoration in humbler homes, where the more readily available 'earth' colours were used. This form of wall decoration continued to be popular, especially in minor houses, for several centuries – sometimes in the form of 'pictures' or sometimes in a more formal manner [pl. 9].

9. Stencilled fleur-de-lis of the late fifteenth century decorate the wattle and daub walls of this room in Bradley Manor. The striped painted 'curtain' next to the window is also from the late fifteenth or early sixteenth century.

From the middle of the thirteenth century heraldry played an increasingly important part in the field of decoration. Shields and coats of arms, not only provided recognition on the field of battle and in tournaments, they were also excellent material for decorative use on walls, in wall hangings and tapestries, on plate and in stained glass [pl. 5]. The simple devices and colours of the early arms and crests made them particularly suitable as repetitive patterns. The use of arms in this way also proclaimed the importance and grandeur of the family concerned.

Tapestry and wall hangings of various materials from coarse linen to the finest silk were in common use by the middle of the fourteenth century and are featured in countless wills and inventories of the period. They provided a luxurious and comfortable alternative to wall paintings and had the added convenience of being easily portable. The kings and nobles of the Middle Ages led a peripatetic life, moving from one to another of their great and often far-flung possessions. The comparatively little amount of furniture that would have been in use in even a grand medieval household was movable and would have accompanied the owner. It was the textiles that provided the glamorous, rich colours and the general air of luxury that we see illustrated in medieval manuscripts, miniatures and Books of Hours [pls 6, 10, 11]. The humblest

wall hangings were known as 'stained cloths' and consisted of canvas or linen or, in grander houses, worsted cloths painted with scenes. These 'stained cloths' sometimes formed part of what was known as a 'chamber' – a term more generally applied to tapestry and silk or embroidered hangings. A 'chamber' would consist of any number of hangings in matching or different colours and materials, bed curtains and coverlets, cushions and seat coverings – these latter were loose pieces of material for placing on seats or benches and were called bancoves or bankers; dorsars were similar but hung over the backs of chairs. These different elements would be carefully integrated to present an over-all decorative effect.

Floors could also be decorated with tiles [pl. 10] in various designs – originally they were made by using a stamp with a depressed pattern that was then filled with clay of another colour. The vast majority of thirteenth century tiles are red inlaid with white. The technique of making inlaid tiles was probably brought to England from France in the second quarter of the thirteenth century and was carried on, to begin with, under royal patronage. By the middle of the century floors depicting figures were being designed, such as that in the Westminster chapter house. In the fourteenth century floor tiling became widespread. Eleanor of Castile is credited with having introduced carpets to England. However, when she came to Westminster in 1255 she found her floors already 'carpeted', but this form of floor covering was rare and only found in the richest households. For several centuries carpets were mainly displayed in the form of table covers.

10. A late-fifteenth-century manuscript shows John of Portugal entertaining John of Gaunt. The 'canopy of state' in rich blue and gold and green and gold silks appears in front of the hooded fireplace, oddly placed between two windows. The floor is tiled in three colours. (British Library, London.)

A large range of textiles was available for furnishing – cotton was imported from the Mediterranean and Asia and was woven with home-produced linen to make fustian used for bedding. Linen cloth was produced in England but was also imported. Silk was brought in as thread as well as in an enormous variety of woven silk cloth such as cendal, a lightweight plain weave material available in many colours, samite which was heavier with a twill weave or, most luxurious of all, velvet woven mainly in Italy and used for both clothes and furnishings. However, the most widely used fibre was undoubtedly wool of which England was an enormous producer and exporter both in the raw state and as cloth. In 1337, when Edward III was in the Low Countries seeking to employ mercenaries he was so impressed by the Flemish cloth workers that he invited a number of them to come and settle in England and this gave a tremendous new impetus to the wool trade. The other great export in the field of the decorative arts was embroidery in silk and gold thread known as *Opus Anglicanum*; this was renowned throughout Europe and highly prized. Although much of this embroidery was designed for church use, and it is this that survives, it was also used for dress and furnishings such as the bed belonging to the widow of the Black Prince who had died in 1376. This was red velvet 'embroidered with ostrich feathers of silver and heads of leopards of gold, with boughs and leaves of silver issuing out of their mouths'. A very wide variety of colours was employed for furnishing textiles and there are frequent references to blanchet (white), bluet (blue), burnet (brown), green, paonaz (peacock colour), russet, violet, scarlet and many, many others.

The grandest and richest households used great scenes of tapestry to cover the walls of their houses and castles and most of these were imported from France and the Low Countries, the most famous coming from Arras in the province of Artois [pls 11, 15]. In fact, arras became the generic term often used for tapestry. Some tapestry was made in London, where the Ordinances of the Trade of Tapiciers are dated 1331, but these weavers were in rivalry to the 'trade of Alien Weavers' – those craftsmen who had been brought to England earlier in the century by Edward III. The weaving of tapestry was very strictly controlled; for instance we read of Katherine Duchewoman being brought before the Masters of the Trade of Tapiciers in London, accused of making a piece of false work after the manner of work of Arras; she had made it of linen thread beneath, but covered with wool above, to the deceit of the people. It was adjudged false and burnt.

Tapestries were often woven to fit a particular room or hall, and within the scheme would be door coverings to keep out draughts. The hangings were attached to the walls by rings, but as they were moved from house to house they were ruthlessly cut to fit the differing dimensions, window openings, and so on, and very few tapestries survive in the position for which they were designed. One of the exceptions in England is the magnificent late-fifteenth-century tapestry depicting the Assumption of the Virgin with Apostles and the kneeling figures of Henry VII and his queen that hangs in St. Mary's Hall, Coventry. This hall was built in the mid- fourteenth cen-

11. King Alphonso V of Aragon kneels on a rug on the tiled floor of this miniature, *c.*1450. The circular hanging above the bed is called a sparver. The walls are lined with a hunting tapestry. (British Library, London.)

tury as a guildhall, and the tapestry, although later, was commissioned for the position in which it still hangs. Many different themes were represented in tapestry, from scenes of battle to courtly love as well as 'histories' and stories from the Bible. The original cartoon from which the tapestry was woven would be used again and again, sometimes over a very long period and with various adaptations, for instance in order to bring the clothes up to date.

The use of hangings appears to have started at the upper end of the hall to make the dais more comfortable and less draughty. Very soon these hangings were used as a canopy over the seat of the most important personage [pl. 10] – it has been plausibly suggested that the canopy was originally invented as protection against bird droppings. Certainly birds would have invaded the great hall through the smoke louvres in the roof. However, the canopy assumed an extra function in medieval times by emphasizing the importance of the seigneur – a symbolic function that continued in the form of canopies over thrones for many centuries. The bed, by far the most expensive piece of furniture in a medieval household, was also canopied and the curtains, of material or tapestry and hung on wooden rails, would be gathered into bags at the corners when not in use [pl. 6]. Bed hangings were rich and beds were well supplied with linen and pillows. For instance, in 1434 Joan Bergavenny left 'A bed of gold swans, the tapestry of green, with bunches of flowers of divers kinds, two pairs of sheets of Rayes [linen from Rennes], a pair of fustaynes, six pair of other sheets, six pair of blankets, six mattresses, six pillows, and the cushions and bancoves that belong to the bed'. In houses of lesser importance the bed was made up on the floor, and at night the hall was converted into a dormitory for the accommodation of strangers or visitors, both sexes sleeping there. It was the duty of the groom of the chambers to provide clean rushes and straw for the floors and the pallets.

Apart from the bed, furniture was scarce. Chests or coffers were most usual and were used for moving goods as well as for storage. The technique of panel construction had been introduced into furniture design in the mid-thirteenth century and this was to have a considerable effect, not only on the making of chests and chairs but also on the construction of wainscot, whence the term panelling derives. Chairs were not common. Any there were would most often be used as chairs of state – under the canopy. For instance, an inventory of 1466 mentions 'A chaire of astate of yren, covered with purpell satyn furred, and a case of lether therto'. The 'case of lether' would have been for protection when the chair was not in use and gives some idea of the value put on such a chair. Benches were for ordinary use and dining tables were just boards on trestles. Also in the hall would be a cupboard, in its original form of open shelves, on which would be displayed plate – cups, flagons and dishes. This again was designed to impress and to display wealth, which would often be in this form rather than in coin. The cupboard was sometimes placed in the bay or oriel window in the hall.

It was the hall that was to provide the greatest tests of skill for the carpenter. At first he was occupied with the structural problem of spanning the ever-increasing size of the great halls and so he was less concerned with the decoration of the structure. Early in the fourteenth century simple forms of decoration began to appear in the treatment of the wind braces of the roof and these struts were formed into the familiar Gothic patterns of trefoils and quatrefoils [pl. 13]. But by 1399 Hugh Herland's majestic roof over Westminster Hall was finished [pl. 12]. Not only does the huge span of $67\frac{1}{2}$ feet (20.6m) represent an incredible advance in timber construction, but the decoration of the roof is equally awe inspiring, the delicate tracery rivalling the stone carving of the great cathedrals. The timber was pared down to the minimum essential to ensure structural stability, which not only lessened the weight but the resultant 'moulding' of each element lightened the visual effect of the whole roof.

The skills of the carpenter were next displayed on the hall screen. Initially the screen was a simple partition erected for purely practical purposes at the end of the hall opposite the dais with its high table. At this end the five doors – the front door and the door to the courtyard and one each to buttery, pantry and kitchen corridor – must have created a source of almost continual draught. The screen with its two openings provided at least a partial remedy. It also gave a perfect opportunity for elaborate decoration in the form of carving [pl. 13], which was probably painted as well, following the example of church screens. Where ecclesiastical and secular practice ran parallel was in the contemporaneous introduction of the gallery in halls and the rood loft in churches, both situated above the screen and both providing a platform for musical performance.

The hall screen extended to the same height as the wainscot or panelling and formed a break approximately half-way up the wall. The windows in a number of halls were positioned above the panelling.

12. The transformation of William Rufus's Westminster Hall was undertaken by Richard II at the end of the fourteenth century. The king's mason, Henry Yevele, and the chief carpenter, Hugh Herland, worked on the plans for two years before construction started in 1394. Twenty-six carved angels decorate the hammer beams.

The emergent skills of the joiner and carpenter became more and more apparent towards the end of the fifteenth century. The introduction of a vertical rib into the centre of a panel terminating at the top and bottom in ogival curves was first evident in furniture but was soon adopted for panelling. This 'wavy woodwork' as it was called, with the additional carving of more ribs, was the precursor of what the Victorians were to re-christen 'linenfold' panelling. Ceilings were also introduced at this time. Early examples were of thin tongued and grooved boarding, the decoration being added in the form of applied mouldings dividing the ceiling into small squares. The addition of a cornice to cover the joint between the wall and the ceiling provided an opportunity for further embellishment [pl. 14].

Two vital conditions, however, were required in order for these expensive and time-consuming essays in decorative treatment to flourish – a settled country and a stable economy. The end of the Wars of the Roses in 1485 and the establishment of the Tudor dynasty provided both conditions.

Unfortunately, only a fragmented and largely colourless view of the period has reached us, much having been destroyed through ignorance. The nineteenth- and twentieth-century fashion for emphasizing the timber structure by painting the wood black and the plaster infill white gives a wholly false impression of the medieval interior. As recently discovered wall paintings have revealed, the craftsman or artist painted indiscriminately over both timber frame and plaster alike. It is unlikely that medieval man would recognize our naive, black and white 'Christmas card' view of his world.

13. This movable free-standing screen rather ineffectually masks the now blocked up doorways to the pantry and buttery – the three finials are later additions. The hall at Rufford Old Hall, *c.*1500, is decorated with elaborate woodwork including a hammer beam roof, unusual in a comparatively small room.

14. The great chamber of the Bede House, Lyddington, was used by the bishop of the see for receiving. The late-fifteenth-century windows bear the arms of various bishops. The exceptional carved early-sixteenth-century cornice was once richly coloured and the walls were hung with tapestries – the hatchments are a later addition.

2

TUDOR COMFORT AND RENAISSANCE DETAIL

Henry VII had laboriously established a peaceful and economically stable country and on his death in 1509 he was fittingly commemorated by the great tomb erected by his son. Henry VIII employed the Italian sculptor Pietro Torrigiano to design this monument in Westminster Abbey, and with this great act of patronage he gave England its first sight of that 'rebirth' of classical Roman culture which, since 1840, we know as the Renaissance. It was, sadly, little more than a brief glance at authentic Renaissance decoration. Henry VIII's break with Rome effectively deprived the English of any first-hand knowledge of Italian architecture and decoration for the rest of the sixteenth century.

This information had to be filtered at second hand through France and the Low Countries or at third hand through French or Flemish books. Decorative architectural details from these sources were grafted on to what was, essentially, a late stage of Gothic architecture. The result was a mesalliance but one with a uniquely English character.

The fact that England was an artistic backwater did not inhibit the English from decorating their houses. Stable conditions and the urge for an ever-increasing measure of privacy encouraged both new building and additions and alterations to old property. One of the more important of these alterations was the construction of ceilings in rooms formerly open to the rafters. This not only added an extra floor of accommodation, but also the ceiling itself provided a new surface to decorate [pl. 22]. Another frequent addition at this time was the long gallery. The earliest one still in existence, at the Vyne in Hampshire, was built around 1525. The gallery provided an excellent opportunity for a display of craftsmanship on a large scale, as at the Vyne with its linenfold panelling or, nearly a century later, at Knole [pl. 16]. Such grand examples would seem to presuppose their use as rooms of entertainment despite the long-held belief that they were designed for the purpose of taking exercise in inclement weather. In less important houses the decoration was often minimal and in such cases the galleries may well have been used as dormitories.

Building for defence had been expensive, and the money saved on this now unnecessary function could be used either for added comfort or for aesthetic purposes. The size and number of windows steadily increased throughout the Tudor era. In the fifteenth century most glass had to be imported and was extremely expensive, but towards the end of the sixteenth century there were fifteen glass factories in England and by 1579 it was regarded in law as a fixture, as 'glass fixed by nails to windows, or in any other manner, cannot be moved, for without glass is no perfect house'.

The often elaborate Gothic tracery in early Tudor windows

15. A watercolour, *c.* 1799, of the Painted Chamber, Palace of Westminster, showing the fourteenth-century windows and sixteenth-century ceiling. The rush matting goes up the walls to meet the tapestry hangings as it did in the fifteenth and sixteenth centuries. The fireplace is from the eighteenth century. (Guildhall Library, City of London.)

was superseded by the rectangular shapes formed by simple mullions and transoms. But decorative possibilities of the windows were not ignored. Stained glass retained its popularity and the glass, whether stained or not, was framed in numerous and ingenious patterns [pls 17, 22].

Although the use of flat Tudor arches for windows had all but ceased by the middle of the sixteenth century, they remained fashionable as heads for fireplaces for another fifty years. This persistent use of the Tudor arch in fireplaces may well have been due to its efficient shape – the large opening being higher at the centre than on either side. This would explain why it was sometimes retained within a later superimposed framework of elaborate Renaissance detail. As a vehicle for new fashions in decoration, fireplaces were the secular equivalents of the very elaborate contemporary monu-

16. The decoration of the Cartoon Gallery at Knole was carried out at the very beginning of the seventeenth century while the furniture is from the late seventeenth and early eighteenth century. The 'grotesque' motifs on the pilasters form part of the painted decoration, which cost £100 in 1608.

17. The signing of the peace treaty with Spain in 1604. The large windows, tapestry hangings, elaborate 'grotesque' painting and, above all, the costly oriental carpet on the table show that this meeting was taking place in luxurious surroundings – in fact, Somerset House. (National Portrait Gallery, London.)

ments in churches. They were positive statements of status and wealth. Compressed into this one feature of a room all the newly imported decorative details were flaunted in wood, plaster, stone or marble.

The books which began to appear in some quantity in the mid-1600s were plundered as sources for such decorative details. Vitruvius's book *de Architectura*, written about AD 25, and Sebastiano Serlio's six books of architecture together with John Shute's English version of these authors provided the classical orders. Serlio also offered a profusion of designs for ceilings, doorways, fireplaces and other details. But far more influential were the books by German and Flemish engravers containing designs for strapwork and 'grotesques' [pl. 20].

'Grotesque' or 'antick work' appears as a recurrent theme for the next three hundred years. During the Renaissance, buildings of classical antiquity such as Nero's Golden House built in *c.*AD 65 were discovered underground, yielding both the name (from the Italian word for a cave – *grotta*) and the designs which were to provide Raphael with a source for his decoration of the Vatican Loggia and the Villa Madama, begun in 1517. Despite the idiosyncratic distortion of the animals and some of the human figures which, together with plants, form the major elements of 'grotesque' decoration, the whole effect is one of refinement as opposed to the rather crude contortions of strapwork [pl. 19].

18. Three panels of 'grotesque' and strapwork decoration now at Loseley Hall but thought to have come from Nonsuch Palace – the centre panel when complete contained the device of Catherine Parr, thus these panels must have been made after her marriage to Henry in 1543.

19. Detail of the ceiling of Plate 28. The elaborate decoration uses a limited palette of reds, greens and yellow. The whole surface is divided into panels that are filled with strange half-human figures or delicate arabesques with flowers and exotic birds.

Strapwork first appeared in England when Henry VIII brought over artists from the Continent to decorate Nonsuch Palace at Ewell in Surrey, where building began in 1538. Strapwork [pl. 20], one of the most bizarre but hardly the most beautiful of decorative details, was either carved or, more usually, moulded in plaster. It evokes the scrolling and then cutting of leather or parchment into curious, often weird, shapes. It remained a persistent motif in decoration for almost a century, emerging briefly once more in nineteenth-century Tudor Revivals.

By 1532 the Italian painters Giovanni Batista Rosso and Francesco Primaticcio were at work on the decoration of the palace at Fontainebleau for François I. It would seem that this palace had much the same hypnotic effect on northern Europe as Versailles was to have over a century later. The influence of Rosso's and Primaticcio's 'school' of Fontainebleau was to be seen at Nonsuch by the early 1540s.

Little or nothing of Nonsuch survives – it was demolished in the 1680s. Even the panels of 'grotesques' [pl. 18] that were thought to have come from the palace may in fact have been designed for a more transitory purpose, perhaps for some temporary structure erected for entertainment. The borderline between the permanent and the transient in terms of decoration was constantly being bridged. Toto del Nunziata, who had arrived in England with Bartolomeo Penni around 1520, either of whom may have been responsible for the grotesque panels, certainly worked on the decorations for the royal tents. Indeed, many of the court painters were employed for such purposes. The king's Serjeant Painter, John Brown, assisted by John Rastell and Clement Urmystone, undertook that most lavish of such assignments – the king's pavilion at the Field of the Cloth of Gold. This huge temporary structure was designed to impress Francois I at their historic meeting in 1520 on the borders of the French and the English territory at Calais. It was described at the time as 'the most noble and royall lodgying before seen, for it was a palays'. From such theatrical events it was a simple step to scene painting for the court masques, where devices such as false perspective and the rendering of architecture and sculpture in paint were essential for deceiving the eye – this *trompe-l'œil* became a stock in trade for decorators and has been used ever since.

Holbein displayed this skill in his portrait group of Henry VIII with his wife and parents. Only a cartoon and a copy by another artist now exist of Holbein's painting of *c.*1536, on a wall of the Privy Chamber in Whitehall Palace [pl. 21], but they show one of the earliest examples of grotesque decoration in England. Holbein during his first visit to England had been employed on temporary buildings at Greenwich in celebration of the Anglo-French alliance of 1527, and he was certainly subsequently involved in decorative schemes of a permanent nature. Of the very few designs that exist the one for a fireplace, in particular, shows an extravagant use of Renaissance detail.

20. Two illustrations by Hans Vredeman de Vries (1527–1606) from the huge series of ornamental and architectural prints that he produced and that were endlessly copied by designers. The strapwork and 'cabochon' motifs are very typical of his work.

21. A seventeenth-century copy of Holbein's painting on the walls of the Privy Chamber in Whitehall, destroyed by fire in 1698. It shows Henry VIII, his father and mother and his third wife, Jane Seymour, whom he married in 1536. Notice the splendid carpet, the 'antick' work on the pilasters and the architectural detail in the background.

His name has also been associated with the design of ceilings; whether the magnificent ceiling in the chapel of St. James's Palace is his work or not, it is an extremely sophisticated treatment of this comparatively new area of decoration. The interlocking crosses, octagons and lozenges are defined by moulded ribs. The design is taken from Serlio and in both design and painting it represents a spectacular advance from the ceiling in the parlour at Haddon Hall [pl. 22]. In other equally rare survivals of early Tudor ceilings the beams and, where they are exposed, the intervening joists are carved, but only on the underside, or soffit, where the fine carving can be seen to the best advantage.

By about 1530 the beams themselves were being encased in decoration, with cornice-type mouldings applied to each side and a fretwork of carving fixed to the soffit. The advantage of this was that the carving could be done on the work-bench and then placed in position. This practice inevitably led to finer workmanship, if only because the craftsmen were working under easier and more congenial conditions. This custom was followed increasingly for both fine carving and, in the case of plasterwork, repetitive work that could be cast in moulds.

One additional refinement in construction was the introduction, probably by Henry VIII's foreign workmen, of suspended ceilings whereby not only the joists were covered, but also the main beams. It was, however, more expensive to achieve and in less important rooms and small houses these structural members continued to be left exposed – beams often suffer this exposure today.

22. The ceiling of the parlour at Haddon Hall dates from 1500 and is painted with arms and the Tudor rose on a red and white chequerboard. The wainscot and the windows date from 1545. This is a very complete and typical example of a Tudor living room.

23. The Winter Parlour at Canons Ashby was created to provide a private eating room away from the hall. The panelling was painted in the 1590s with crests of local families set in strapwork against a gold background. The panels below the cornice contain a series of moral inscriptions in Latin.

The development of linenfold panelling between the late fifteenth and early sixteenth century was one of increasingly assured craftsmanship, the fold becoming more and more realistic – even the stitches were simulated by a delicately punched border [pl. 25]. But however intricate and elaborate the carving the total effect of such panelling was one of sobriety.

The wood-carvers, like the plasterers, were soon goaded into elaboration by their patrons, who were anxious, no doubt, to display their 'Renaissance' credentials. Inlaid work in woods such as poplar and bog oak was added to the repertoire [pl. 24] to enrich the architectural details, such as pilasters, as well as the panels themselves. The familiar Renaissance motifs were often indiscriminately mixed up with bands of natural foliage and the inevitable devices of heraldry [pl. 23]. In the medieval hall the panelling only covered the lower half of the walls, but with the introduction of the ceiling it became practicable to

A simple flat ceiling obviously provided a challenge to the Tudors and Jacobeans, who were to pursue complexity with ever increasing vigour. For a time, decorative treatment was restrained. Small mouldings in plaster were used to form simple geometric patterns echoing the earlier examples in wood, but as the full potential of plasterwork decoration was realised, designs of immense complexity were achieved. The ribs in deep relief and intricate form converged at points into pendants which were suspended on wire armatures fixed to the joists. The pendants themselves derived from the carved timber ones in late medieval roofs. Between the ribs, strapwork in lower relief added to the opulent effect [pl. 24].

This progression from the restraint of early Tudor decoration to the unbridled ostentation of the late Elizabethan and the Jacobean period was mirrored in the panelling of rooms.

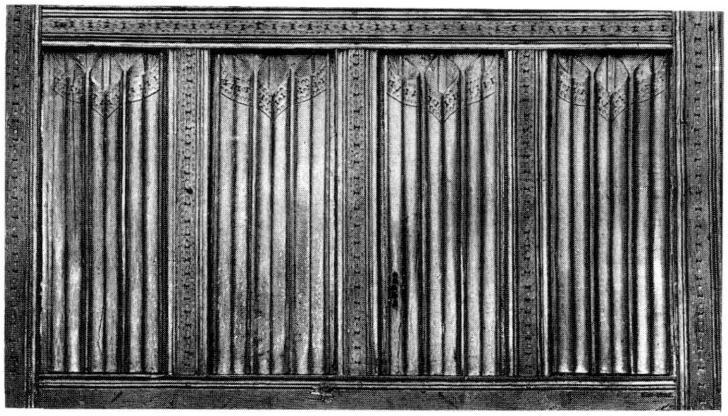

24. The Inlaid Chamber from Sizergh Castle depicted by Joseph Nash in 1849. This room, now in the Victoria and Albert Museum, is elaborately decorated with fine inlaid panels dating from 1568. The ceiling with intricate rib patterns and pendants dates from *c.*1575 and is of the type that became common in late-sixteenth-century houses.

25. Fifteenth-century panelling of the pattern known as linenfold. This very sophisticated version imitates lace edging at the top of each panel. (Victoria and Albert Museum, London.)

26 (*above*). This room in the Little Castle, Bolsover, where building began between 1608 and 1613, illustrates an interesting seventeenth-century medieval revival in the groin vaulting and the hooded fireplace. The panelling and painting above are seventeenth-century in concept as well as execution.

27. The High Great Chamber at Hardwick Hall, *c.*1600, is hung with tapestries for just over half the height; above these is a painted plaster frieze of hunting scenes in deep relief (small real trees are embedded in the plaster). The fireplace incorporates cabochon shapes in strapwork.

28. A highly decorated, if slightly old-fashioned, room of the 1630s in a prosperous merchant's house in a country town. The arabesque painting in the grained panels is varied by the use of the three colours of paint, and the fireplace, with a flat Tudor arch opening,is painted to simulate different stones.

29. The small room called the Bower, at Castle Ashby, was probably originally a dressing-room or closet. The delicate plasterwork, painted panels and fireplace date from the mid-1630s; the daybed is covered in eighteenth-century painted taffeta (pl. 81). Each panel, painted in gold on green, is surmounted by a small landscape view.

extend it to the full height of the room. In many cases, however, a frieze was introduced, possibly to provide a contrast where the panelling was comparatively plain. This plaster surface could then carry the more elaborate decoration in paint of Renaissance themes, landscapes or historical scenes [pls. 26, 27].

By the end of the century the panelling itself was sometimes the subject of bizarre designs where much deeper mouldings delineated panels of eccentric shapes. However, plain square or rectangular panelling was common throughout the period, persisting in smaller houses until the second half of the seventeenth century. It had two important advantages: it was comparatively cheap; and it could be decorated with paint – existing evidence would indicate that it frequently was. Whether in a merchant's house [pl. 28] or a great aristocratic mansion [pl. 29], repetitive devices in panels confirm the widespread use of stencils.

Painting was not confined to panelling. Sometimes paint was used to create the illusion of panelling [pl. 30] and elsewhere the medieval tradition of simulating wall hangings continued and tapestry was imitated in paint [pl. 31]. That these designs were frequently carried out in black and white underlines their source in engravings. The artist paid no attention to the different surfaces on which he was painting – the design itself and perhaps some accompanying text would continue over structural timber and plaster alike. Painted inscriptions or monograms were a common addition to designs and had parallels in post-Reformation church decoration.

Real wall hangings of various kinds continued to be extremely popular but they were no longer moved from house to house because, except for the royal 'Progresses', it was not usual for great households to move about in the way that had been customary in the Middle Ages. In fact, sometimes rooms were built to accommodate existing tapestry rather than the tapestry being commissioned to fit the room [pl. 33]. By the beginning of the sixteenth century there was already a vast quantity of tapestry in England but it continued to be imported from the Low Countries, mostly from Brussels, which had taken over from Tournai as the leading centre of manufacture. Henry VIII had almost a mania for acquiring tapestries, and the inventory taken after his death lists over 2,000 pieces. No other Tudor monarch shared his passion and when, in the 1560s, William Sheldon established the first important English tapestry manufactory in Warwickshire it was not under royal patronage. Some interesting tapestries of very high quality were produced at the Sheldon works, not least a series of large hangings worked as pictorial maps of English counties. They are very finely woven and show much detail, as they were taken from engraved maps. Several of these tapestries survive – there is a beautiful example at Oxburgh Hall – as do some of the smaller pieces, such as cushion covers, which were manufactured by Sheldon. Although the factory continued into the seventeenth century under Sheldon's son and grandson, its importance was soon eclipsed by the Mortlake factory which was founded in 1619 under the patronage of James I.

30. Plain panelling of *c.*1630 painted in *trompe-l'œil* in subtle shades of brown to give a three-dimensional effect. This recent discovery, under many layers of later paint, is at Oakwell Hall.

31. The remains, at Hill Hall, of a wall painted to simulate tapestry with a typical tapestry border, *c.*1570.

32. Part of Elizabethan wall decoration in monochrome at Canons Ashby. Although much damaged it clearly shows windows and a sixteenth-century hanging clock. Notice the column with its capital, the cornice and the flat arches of the windows.

Hangings could also be embroidered or appliquéd as, for instance, the famous wall hangings at Hardwick Hall and the bed curtains (now mounted as wall hangings) at Oxburgh Hall that incorporate needlework panels by Mary, Queen of Scots, and Lady Shrewsbury. Some of the splendid textiles used for hangings, cushions, and bed curtains were originally the property of the Church in the form of copes and chasubles. After the dissolution of the monasteries in 1538 these magnificent textiles were distributed throughout the country, some given as presents and some sold. They were ruthlessly cut up and used for secular purposes – it is conjectured that some of these fabrics were used in the Hardwick hangings and certainly Mary, Queen of Scots, re-used copes and chasubles in her own palaces.

Fine Spanish leather hangings were being imported into England in the latter years of Henry VII's reign, probably as a result of his trade agreement with Spain. The craft of making these extremely rich-looking hangings had been perfected some decades earlier by Moorish workers in Cordoba. Many of these workers migrated to the Low Countries and by the end of the sixteenth century most of the fine Spanish leather imported into England came from the Netherlands. The techniques involved punching the leather and painting and dyeing the surface and also using coloured foil. Leather hangings either illustrated a story in the manner of tapestry or used repetitive patterns incorporating 'grotesque' ornament or heraldic devices.

Smaller country houses were furnished in a simpler and cheaper way. We know of a family named Johnson who moved to Glapthorn Manor in Northamptonshire in 1544 and who ordered some cloth from Antwerp, a 'piece of white say, and another piece of honest sad blue say...both of the best making that is made for hangings'. Say is woollen cloth with a twill weave and was used extensively for hangings and curtains both for beds and, later, for windows. Sad just means a dark shade. The most popular colours, perhaps in honour of the sovereign's red-gold hair, were tawny, orange, yellow, *roy* or *couleur de roy*, which was bright tawny, and other shades such as pear or catherine pear, which was russet red. Other colours, too, had fanciful names, such as popinjay, a mixture of green and blue; plunket or blunket, which was sky blue; and brassel, or brazil, which was red. Mrs Johnson was fond of hangings of painted linens or 'stayned' cloths, also known as 'water-work', as they were cheap and could be extremely decorative [pl. 34]. They were generally painted in imitation of tapestry. On the oak

33. This bedroom at Chastleton, built in the early seventeenth century, was designed to accommodate the three pieces of sixteenth-century Flemish tapestry. The bed is hung with crewel work and the rich plasterwork and fireplace indicate that this was one of the more important rooms in the house.

34. Early-seventeenth-century 'stayned' cloths at Owlpen Manor are a hang-over from a fashion that was popular in the sixteenth century.

floor of her parlour she had green carpet, measuring 15 by $7\frac{1}{2}$ feet (4.5 × 2.25m). The house also boasted several chairs.

By the end of the fifteenth century paper was being freely manufactured all over Europe and this led to the introduction of wallpaper. It made an excellent cheap substitute for hangings of tapestry or leather and some of the first patterns in England seem to have been imitations of costly imported fabrics such as velvet. Also much favoured were patterns incorporating heraldic devices [pl. 35]. They were printed in black and white from wood blocks and were generally pasted straight onto the wall surface.

As we have seen, carpets were imported into England quite early in the Middle Ages and, without doubt, the Crusaders would have seen, admired and perhaps even brought back with them Persian and Turkey carpets. The more usual floor covering had been rushes and bents (sweet-smelling wild plants) and this custom continued into the sixteenth century – Cardinal Wolsey ordered the rushes to be changed every day at Hampton Court but this was extraordinarily extravagant. Wolsey also liked carpets, and in 1518 he 'requested' a gift from the Venetian ambassador in return for trading concessions: he received seven Damascene carpets as a joint gift from the ambassador and the Venetian merchants then in London. However, more were demanded, and in October 1520 sixty further carpets arrived from Venice via Antwerp – they were graciously accepted and the cardinal inspected them one by one. These would have been oriental carpets imported to Venice, then the trading centre of the eastern Mediterranean and Adriatic. Many were used as table carpets, a practice that was to continue for at least another hundred years [pl. 17].

Carpets and coverings for tables and cupboards were usual in the fifteenth and sixteenth centuries and could vary enormously from the luxurious imported carpets such as Cardinal Wolsey's to the quite humble 'dornix' or 'darnix', which was a woollen cloth, often striped or with a small pattern. The name, which occurs frequently in inventories, is a corruption of Tournai, where this type of cloth is supposed to have originated. Worn tapestry was also often cut down to make carpets for furniture. Carpets specifically for use on floors were generally called foot carpets.

During the Tudor years the use of rushes on the floor gradually died out except in very primitive country areas, where the custom lingered on into the nineteenth century. The natural progression was from rushes to rush matting and this became a popular floor covering [pl. 37], as it is today. By the 1550s

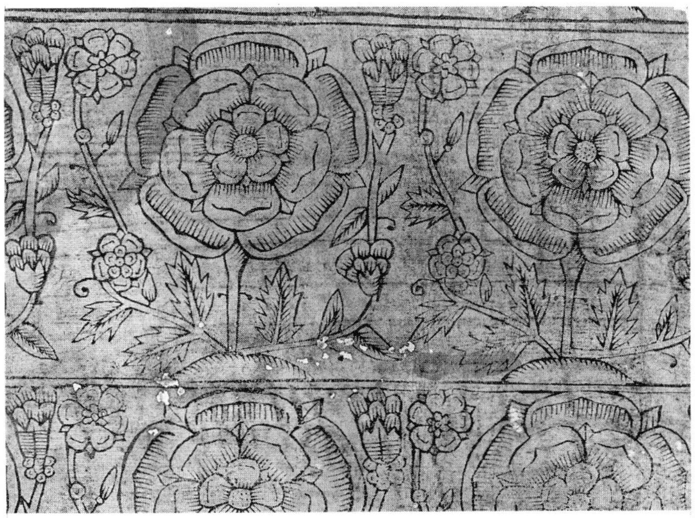

floors were made of wooden planking, generally of oak. In the important apartments of grander houses stone was used, sometimes of different colours laid in patterns.

Imported oriental carpets were imitated in the form of Turkey work which started in England at this time [pl. 36]. This was made of hand-knotted wool, generally based on a canvas backing, in patterns imitating Turkey carpets. It was, in general, quite coarse with strong colours. Towards the end of the sixteenth and throughout the seventeenth century it was largely used for upholstery on seat furniture – in particular for chairs known as back stools, which were, literally, stools with added backs [pl. 38].

One result of the comparative calm of this period was that

35. Woodblock-printed lining paper, *c.*1550, with a simple repeat pattern of the Tudor rose.

36. Detail of a sixteenth-century carpet in the Victoria and Albert Museum. This is English 'Turkey work' in imitation of an oriental carpet.

interior decoration tended to rely less on the use of textiles and more on fixtures and fittings. Rather more furniture was introduced and was not necessarily designed to be movable – for example, eating tables instead of consisting of a board and trestles now had fixed legs and stretchers. As the work of the joiner became more accomplished furniture became more sophisticated and was decorated with lavish carving. This was seen, in particular, in the design of important beds. No longer was the bed a very simple, and often demountable, structure relying for effect on beautiful coverings and hangings. Instead it was sturdily constructed of wood – ideally walnut, which was the preferred timber for Tudor furniture, or oak – and the posts, tester and, particularly, the wainscoted headboard were heavily carved [pl. 24]. The headboards generally contained one or more niches for the accommodation of candles and were splendidly decorated, often with classical or biblical subjects that were mostly copied from imported pattern books. Although these beds were still hung with curtains, of rich or humble material depending on the status of the owner, they relied for their effect on the joinery work and carving.

Window curtains were exceptionally rare, and the cold and light were kept out by the use of shutters – curtains, where referred to in inventories, are nearly always connected with beds. The bedroom as such did not exist and the bed, still the most important and certainly the most expensive piece of furniture in the house, took its place in the parlour or great chamber – a custom that continued to the end of the sixteenth century. By which time, the writer William Harrison, writing in the 1570s and 80s says in his *Description of England*, 'The furniture of our houses also exceedeth, and is grown in manner even to passing delicacy, and herein I doo not speak of the nobilitie and gentrie onelie, but likewise of the lowest sort . . . even unto the inferior artificers and manie farmers, who have learned also to garnish their cupboards with plate, their joined beds with tapisterie and silk hangings, and their tables with carpets and fine naperie, whereby the wealth of our countrie dooth infinetely appeare.'

Stools were the normal seat furniture but, by now, were 'joined stools' – put together by a joiner using proper joints. Chairs were few in number but these were panelled and as richly carved as beds, although with wooden seats. The discomfort of wooden seating was largely mitigated by the liberal use of cushions of every shape and size, including very large cushions used for sitting on the floor [pl. 37]. Queen Elizabeth, when she was dying, spent four days sitting on her floor-

37. Queen Elizabeth receiving the Dutch Ambassadors, *c.*1585. This simple room has only one chair with, however, a canopy of state. The floor covering is rush matting with cushions on which recline the ladies-in-waiting. The wall hangings are decorated with flowers and foliage and the ceiling panels are painted. (Staatliche Kunstsammlungen, Kassel.)

Amiral
Waldrun
Ambassadur

cushions and refusing to go to her bed. Much rich embroidery was used, for example, among the goods of the Earl of Leicester, listed in 1583, was 'a large cushion of needlework, the grounde crimson silk wroughte with flowers, of gold, silver and greene silke, fringed with golde and silke, lyned with crimson satten, with . . . buttons and tasselles at the corners'. As well as providing comfortable seating, cushions played an important part in the scheme of decoration. Damask and velvet were favourite materials, but even in wealthy households, economies were made as at Leicester House, where in 1588 four square cushions were listed 'all of blacke and purple figured satin, and made of an old gowne of my Lady's'.

By 1547 we hear of richly upholstered and painted chairs such as this one in the list of Henry VIII's possessions: 'One cheir of wood turned and painted walnut-tree colour and parcell guilte the seate and backe covered with blacke vellat embroidered with Venice gold and fringed with yellowe and blacke silke'. These painted and upholstered chairs were at first confined to royal palaces, although later they became more plentiful. The X shape, with the frame completely covered with silk or velvet, also came into favour. The seat was webbed, with loose cushions matching the frame, which was trimmed with gold or silver fringe [pl. 48]. The fabrics employed were often heavily embroidered and matched the bed furniture, foreshadowing the decorative schemes of the latter half of the seventeenth century.

At the same time as the joiners were carving elaborate beds, tables and panelling, another opportunity arose for them to extend their skills with the introduction around 1600 of the open-well staircase. It also provided a further agreeable chance for ostentatious display, once the structural problems that had previously held the staircase in the bondage of supporting walls had been overcome. Every available surface was carved with grotesque or strapwork ornament and every newel post was surmounted by complex finials or heraldic beasts [pl. 39]. A particular feature of these staircases was the turned balusters. The technique of turning wood was practised for centuries before Christ but its use for both staircases and furniture was only introduced into England in the sixteenth century.

Although Renaissance ideas reached England in the sixteenth century, it was only the decorative details that were seized upon with such avidity. The exuberant employment of this Renaissance ornament became technically more proficient during the period but progressively more insular, through either ignorance of, or disdain for, its proper context. By the last decades of Elizabeth's reign this resulted in incredibly opulent and perhaps rather vulgar interiors with every available surface carved, painted or extravagantly plastered.

After the break with Rome it was still possible to travel abroad, even to Italy, but it was both an arduous undertaking and officially discouraged. James I became king in 1603, and in actively encouraging closer links with the Continent fostered the first real understanding of design in architecture and decoration, based on the classical rules of order and proportion.

38. This portrait of the Countess of Derby, *c.*1630, is in the Victoria and Albert Museum. The window glazing is one of many complicated patterns that remained in favour for some hundred years and the floor covering is still rush matting. The back stool is covered with a richly figured silk and embellished with silver fringe.

39. The open-well staircase at Knole was constructed between 1605 and 1608 and the *grisaille* painting is of the same date. Here the classical orders are used in their correct sequence: Tuscan for the ground floor, Ionic at first floor with Corinthian directly above. The turned balusters are echoed on the wall in paint.

IPSIQVE TAMEN TIBI MORTVVS ESTO
VITALE EST SPIRITVS INTVS ALAT
CORPVS PRATA DOMOS VIVI CENSETO SEPVLCRA
PECCATIS VLLA SIT INDE TVIS
MORIENS ÆTERNVM VIVERE PERGE
TETRA DIES MVLTIS SIC ERIT ALMA TIBI

3

PALLADIAN ORDER AND BAROQUE SPLENDOUR

In the last years of Elizabeth's reign, Inigo Jones, one of the few men in England capable of assimilating the essence of the Renaissance architecture, made his first trip to Italy. His early sketches for the costumes and scenery for the court masques [pl. 41] show him to be as much a European as an Englishman. By the time of his second visit to Italy in 1613 he was ready to concentrate on buildings. As a result he transformed English architecture, and the classical disciplines of order and proportion he introduced had an obvious effect on decoration [pl. 40].

Elizabethan and Jacobean builders tended towards a regular disposition of the elements of rooms – such as windows and fireplaces – to match the symmetrical design for their exteriors. But these elements were often trapped in a maze of detail. Initially the influence of Inigo Jones operated at only the most exalted level of patronage. Jones's precepts were not followed outside court circles until after the Restoration of the monarchy, with the exception of a few isolated examples built just before or during the Commonwealth.

The shape of the windows and the regularity of their disposition, both externally and internally, was one of the most notable features that Jones introduced. The vertical, rectangular window and the resulting spaces between windows gave a more even distribution of light and affected the arrangement of furniture and the development of curtaining. The single mullion and transom windows and the carefully propor-

40 (*opposite*). The strong architectural decoration of this room at Haynes Grange may possibly have been designed by Inigo Jones, if not it can only have been designed by someone under his influence. However, the strapwork in the main frieze and the frieze of the fireplace is uncharacteristic of Jones.

41 (*above*). Inigo Jones's design for the masque *Oberon, the Fairy Prince*, 1611. If Jones had not quite mastered classical architecture at this early date he certainly knew enough to incorporate classical decorative detail in his designs. (Chatsworth House.)

42. An English lady's bedchamber, *c.*1640. The box bed is of the type fashionable during the first half of the century. The dressing table is covered with a fringed cloth and on top of this a *toilette* of linen edged with lace (thus the word toilet). The portraits are hung on the tapestry lining the walls. (Pepys Library, Magdalene College, Cambridge.)

tioned spaces between them were first seen on Jones's Lodging at Newmarket for Henry, Prince of Wales, and more prominently on his Banqueting House in Whitehall, built for James I and completed in 1622. The introduction of the longer sash windows in the 1680s increased the light but did not affect the relationship of windows to wall. Almost certainly Jones would have used sash windows. Doors and fireplaces were as carefully positioned as windows so that for the first time the important features of architectural decoration were brought into a controlled and orderly framework below the new compartmented ceiling which Jones had introduced [pl. 43].

Having established the firm principles of classical building, Inigo Jones might have been expected to adhere to them in

architectural decoration rather more than he did. When he arrived in Italy on his second visit, Baroque features in architecture and decoration were about to coalesce into a style. Already by 1614 he had made it plain where the classical rules might be bent a little: 'And to saie trew all thes composed ornamentes the wch Proceed out of ye aboundance of dessignes and wear brought in by Mihill Angell and his followers in my oppignion do not well in sollid Architecture and ye facciati of houses, but in gardens loggis stucco or ornamentes of chimnie piecces or the innerparts of hoases thes composisiones ar of necesety to be youced, for as outwardly euery wyse ma[n] carrieth a graviti in Publicke Places, whear ther is nothing els looked for, & yt inwardly hath his immaginacy set free, and sumtimes licenciously flying out, as nature hirsealf doeth often tymes stravagantly, to dellight, amase us sumtimes moufe us to laughter, sumtimes to contemplatio[n] and horror, So in architecture ye outward ornamentes oft to be sollid, proporsionable according to the rulles, masculine and unaffected.'

Inigo Jones was careful, however, to keep such 'licencious' decoration under strict control. The architectural *trompe-l'œil* or *quadratura* indicated in one panel of his ceiling design [pl. 43] was to become an important constituent of Baroque decoration later in the century. But it was kept firmly in place within the architectural ribs. Even Rubens's great Baroque paintings for the ceiling of the Banqueting House were confined within the framework of Jones's compartments.

The coved ceiling, which Jones also introduced, was only used for the grandest rooms as, not surprisingly, it was considered a waste of space. The coved ceilings of the Double and Single Cube rooms at Wilton [pl. 44] take up one third of the total height. Jones's coves and compartments were suitable for only the most palatial of houses at this time and in any case the political upheaval in the middle of the century effectively put a stop to the building of such houses. Nor did the Civil War followed by the Commonwealth do anything to advance the skills of craftsmanship.

The available skills of the craftsman were no match for Jones's genius, whose designs were infinitely more sophisticated than the rather crude forms of decoration practised both before and during much of the time he was working. It was not until the 1670s that the carvers and plasterers could produce work worthy of the designs they were expected to carry out. The increase in their skills was largely due to the standards laid down by Christopher Wren, who became Surveyor General in 1669, and set about reorganizing the Office of Works.

43. This design by Inigo Jones for a ceiling, ascribed to the Prince's Lodging at Newmarket, dates from as early as 1618–19 and shows the result of his studies of classical architecture on his second visit to Italy in 1613. Note the *trompe-l'œil* effect in the panel below the central one.

44. Inigo Jones's pupil and assistant John Webb was responsible for the redecoration of the Double Cube room at Wilton after the fire of 1647 (possibly with advice from Jones). As at the earlier Haynes Grange, this room is panelled in pine but here painted and gilded.

VNG·IE·SER
VIRAY

45. The staircase at Eltham Lodge shows turned balusters (in the foreground) and one of the earliest versions of a balustrade with panels of acanthus foliage carved out of pinewood blocks 4 inches (10cm) thick and originally painted off-white. The illustration shows the balustrade grained and an extremely rare *trompe-l'œil* wallpaper. Both graining and wallpaper are of the early nineteenth century.

After 1670, ceilings relied almost exclusively on the plasterer for their decorative effects. The rigid rectangular nature of Jones's compartments and architectural motifs was replaced by the naturalistic forms of shells, leaves and flowers formed into garlands or running borders of decoration [pl. 46]. The introduction of a quicker-drying and harder plaster enabled the plasterers to undercut the surface to an extraordinary degree and this, together with individually moulded flowers and fruit fixed to wire armatures, gave an astonishing depth to the plasterwork.

Some of the finest plasterwork in post-Restoration houses was reserved for the ceilings over staircases, which followed the plan of the Jacobean open-well staircase. Inigo Jones's beautiful, circular staircase with its delicate wrought-iron balustrade, at the Queen's House, Greenwich, was so in advance of its time that it had no influence on the design of staircases for at least fifty years. Jones's designs for turned balusters had a more immediate and lasting effect. The type he introduced, originally conceived by Michelangelo and later used by Andrea Palladio, became a standard pattern from the middle of the century. There are numerous examples in houses of every size – carved, painted and gilded in the grander houses and plain oak versions in smaller houses. They were also sometimes used for secondary staircases and even for the upper flights of main stairs, when the ascent to the principal rooms on the first floor was balustraded with panels of carved, naturalistic ornament that complemented the plasterwork of the ceiling [pl. 45].

These elaborately carved panels derived from those of strapwork that were still in evidence in the 1630s when the staircase at Ham House was installed. This early example has trophies of arms while virtually all subsequent ones had naturalistic foliage. The staircase at Ham House was grained and gilded but it is not certain whether other staircases of the period were similarly treated. In some instances the use of different woods together suggests that certain parts, at least, were designed to be painted or grained. Although pine, ash or oak were chosen for the carved balustrades, the steps were invariably of oak, as was most panelling.

The small square or rectangular panels of Elizabethan and Jacobean oak panelling continued to be used, particularly in smaller houses, for much of the first half of the century. Pine was only used in special instances where the panelling was designed to be painted. As with other features, the design of panelling had to conform to an architectural principle. Pilasters had already been used [pl. 40] and in the 1630s a continuous break at dado level made an early appearance. By 1640 the design of panelling was governed by a classical 'Order' and divided into three parts where the area from the floor to the dado rail represented the plinth of a column; the wall surface above, the shaft; and the cornice, the capital [pl. 44]. In the Double Cube room at Wilton the panels play a secondary role in the decorative scheme. The actual moulding round the panels is comparatively insignificant amid the exuberance of the rest of the carved decoration. This is in contrast to the panelling favoured after the Restoration [pl. 50], which was framed with a deep bolection moulding and was usually made in oak, even in smaller houses. But the design retained the principle of the classical 'Order'. Enrichment was confined to the carving of the door architraves, which displayed natural forms such as acanthus leaves on the bolection moulding, an even bolder version of which was carried through to the marble or stone surround to the fireplace.

The quiet, sombre classical interiors of post-Restoration houses were comfortable and unostentatious. Architects like

46. The saloon at Sudbury Hall displays magnificent craftsmanship of the 1670s. The carving is by Edward Pierce and the plasterwork by Bradbury and Pettifer. The ceiling painting, by Louis Laguerre, was added in 1691. The line of the dado is much more obvious here than in the illustration of the Double Cube room (pl. 44).

Roger Pratt, having assimilated the classical rules that Inigo Jones had laid down for them, were able to concentrate on more practical problems. Their houses were planned in a more compact and thoroughly sensible way. The rooms were no longer strung out in draughty wings, only accessible from each other, but were arranged on either side of a central corridor. In England, and in the American colonies, this type of house, in its less grand form, continued to be built throughout the period.

The Baroque style, which originated in Rome about 1620 and reached England in the 1670s, was by its very nature a palatial style. Inigo Jones, in the passage already quoted (p. 42), refers to the sensations that can be induced through the design of 'the inner parts of houses'. Implicit in his suggestions are many ingredients of the Baroque – a desire to impress, to exaggerate, to surprise, even to shock. He also implies a sense of drama and emotion. During the next thirty-five years architects and designers sought to express these effects in architecture and, perhaps even more, in decoration. They achieved this through illusion, elaboration and complexity, a sense of scale and drama and deliberately visible extravagance.

Illusion, complexity and extravagance were all brought to bear on the treatment of panelling – the cheaper pine was substituted for oak painted to create the illusion of expensive wood and marble and then gilded with gold leaf to enhance the rich effect of different materials used together. Grained or marbelized bolection mouldings were used to frame paintings of scenes [pl. 51] or rock-work [pl. 50] and panels of leather [pl. 49] or lacquer [pl. 52]. In the State Drawing Room at Chatsworth the richness of the carved cornice is carried through to the area above the fireplace where the carving is applied as a frame to the inlaid work of the oval panel [pl. 47]. At this time carving reached its highest point, particularly in the case of applied carving, which was usually in lime wood and invariably composed of naturalistic forms. While Grinling Gibbons [pl. 48] was undoubtedly the greatest exponent, others such as Samuel Watson, John Selden and Edward Pierce executed work of the finest quality.

Bolection moulding, perhaps because it was bold enough, seems to be entirely appropriate in both the restrained Restoration decoration and in the great Baroque interiors. It was perhaps the only element that remained common to both schemes of decoration. Plasterwork on ceilings, for example, was phased out in favour of a completely different treatment and one that would extend over the walls as well – illusionist painting [pl. 56]. One of the finest craftsmen in plasterwork,

47. State Drawing-Room at Chatsworth, 1690-4. The ceiling was painted by Louis Laguerre. The Mortlake tapestries, woven about 1630 were framed with new mouldings in the nineteenth century. The English needlework carpet was made about 1710.

48. Grinling Gibbons's carving in limewood at Petworth was carried out between 1689 and 1692 and is probably his finest surviving work. Gibbons's incredible feats of carving should be compared to the crudeness of the carving of the drops in the Double Cube room at Wilton (pl. 44).

49 (*above left*). The chinoiserie panels in this small late-seventeenth-century room are in painted or japanned leather. The moulding would probably have been marbelized like those at Hill Court (pl. 50).

50 (*left*). Room at Hill Court, 1705. This detail shows the bold bolection moulding with raised and fielded panels. The mouldings and dado rails are marbelized while the panels are painted in reds, browns and creams to represent rockwork. The stiles and rails are painted with chinoiserie scenes in tones of brown with cream highlights to simulate lacquer.

51 (*above*). Painted panels by Robert Robinson, 1696, now in the Sir John Cass School. The exotic scenes fancifully depicted in this room range from the Americas to the Far East and foreshadow the later Rococo chinoiserie. Robinson probably also designed tapestry for John Vanderbank (pl. 58).

52 (*opposite*). In the Lacquer Cabinet at Drayton a coromandel lacquer screen was cut up and fitted as panels, probably around 1700. John Evelyn noted a similar use of lacquer screens in 1679.

Edward Goudge, complained in 1702 'for want of money occasioned by the War, and by the use of ceiling painting, the employment which hath been by chiefest pretence hath been always dwindling away, til now its just come to nothing'.

The first and greatest Baroque rooms were, fittingly, at Windsor, where Hugh May remodelled part of the castle to provide new state apartments for Charles II. In 1675 the Italian Antonio Verrio began to paint a series of ceilings for the state rooms. Hugh May reintroduced the cove for these rooms, which Verrio also painted. On two staircases and in both the chapel and St. George's Hall the walls were drawn into the scheme. In the chapel Verrio's *trompe-l'œil* painting merged into Grinling Gibbons's carving, leaving the spectator unsure as to which parts of the decoration were three-dimensional and which were painted [pls. 53, 54].

The opening up of rooms to seemingly endless space through illusionist painting was accomplished by other artists as well as Verrio. The Frenchmen Louis Laguerre and Louis Cheron, the Fleming Gerard Lanscroon, and the Englishman James Thornhill were among the most prolific. This decorative treatment was often reserved for the staircase hall for the very good reason that it provided the painter with the largest and highest area of wall in a house, although Baroque rooms in general were noticeably higher than those of earlier periods. In the majority of these halls the staircases themselves were of stone rising from a stone floor and with a balustrade of wrought ironwork [pl. 56].

Although Inigo Jones had designed a black and white patterned floor to echo the ceiling for the hall of the Queen's House at Greenwich, it was not until nearly the end of the century that marble floors patterned in black and white became fashionable. This kind of floor was extremely expensive and only a possibility for houses such as Petworth House, where there is an elaborate and very complex example in the hall – a pattern that derives, in part, from *Cours complet d'architecture* by C.A. d'Aviler, published in France in 1691. This book contained a number of designs for floors and was mercilessly pillaged [pl. 55] for at least the next hundred years.

53 (*opposite*). Painted room at Canons Ashby, *c.*1717. The *trompe-l'œil* painting in this room was probably carried out by Elizabeth Creed – a gifted amateur and cousin of the owner of the house. The panels are unusual for this date in not being raised and fielded.

54 (*above*). Detail of Plate 53. The cornice and architrave are flat pieces of timber as are the pilasters with their cut-out capitals which give the illusion of being three-dimensional by *trompe-l'œil* painting. The colours in this room were fashionable in Baroque interiors.

55. An illustration from *Various Kinds of Floor Decoration represented both in Plan and Perspective Being useful Designs for Ornamenting the Floors of Halls, Rooms, Summer Houses, etc.* by John Carwitham, published in 1739.

Until the mid-eighteenth century, timber floors were, in the main, meant to be seen and the best quality ones were made of oak, although deal was imported from the mid-seventeenth century. The boards were carefully chosen and laid but these plain floors were not polished – the correct way of cleaning was set out in an eighteenth-century book of housekeeping: 'Sand and Water, after all Spots and Stains are got out, cleans Boards better than any thing, gives them the right colour, and shews the Grain, which is the Beauty of a Board.' Parquet was introduced from France in the 1650s [pl. 60] and was still being laid in the early years of the next century. This, naturally, was meant to be polished. Even more elaborate marquetry was sometimes used on staircase landings and in other special positions.

Traditional rush matting went on being used as a floor covering, but finer, patterned mats were imported from North Africa and the East. In 1666, Samuel Pepys noted, that he was presented with 'a very fine African matt'. Mats of this kind were often used in bedchambers to lay under the beds in place of a carpet.

Oriental carpets were imported by the East India Company and were used as table carpets, as they had been in the previous century, although inventories show that Turkey carpets were sometimes used on the floor – for instance, in the 1654 inventory of Ham House 'A large turkie foot carpet' is listed in what was then the chief apartment on the ground floor. This is by no means an isolated instance and, as already mentioned, Turkey work continued to be made in England through the seventeenth century.

The granting of a charter to the East India Company at the very beginning of the seventeenth century – their first trading venture was in 1601 – marked the start of the interest in all things Eastern that became a feature of the decoration of the period. The company was originally formed to trade with the East, exchanging English woollen cloth for spices. As might be expected, this proved unacceptable to the inhabitants of the tropical Spice Islands and a three-way trade soon developed, with India providing painted and printed cottons, called pintadoes or chintes, in exchange for woollen cloth. These chintzes – so called after the Hindi *chint* meaning variegated – were then traded for spices. Naturally enough, some cottons found their way back to England and were immediately appreciated for their colourful and colourfast properties [pl. 57].

English trade with the East increased enormously during the second half of the seventeenth century after the Anglo-Dutch wars and the consequent limitations placed on the Dutch East India Company and Dutch shipping. Chinese lacquer and porcelain, tortoiseshell, shells of all kinds, ivory, and cotton cloth were an important part of the cargoes from the East. All these goods tended to go by the generic description of 'Indian', as they were loaded from Indian ports. For instance, Samuel Pepys had himself painted in what he called an 'India' gown, in fact, cotton. He also bought some cotton which he called 'chinke' with which to hang the walls of his wife's study.

The Indian cottons or calico, called after Calicut on the Malabar coast where the textiles were collected for shipping, were of various qualities and were woven with coloured stripes or checks or painted and printed. The use of mordants with madder produced fast dyes – an absolute novelty in England. It was not long before the English calico printers had mastered the technique of block printing in a limited range of fast colours – brown, black, purple and the most popular, red. In 1676 a certain William Sherwin was granted a patent for fourteen years 'for a new way of printing broad calicoe' in 'the only true way of East India printing and stayning such kind of goods'. As well as 'Indian' patterns of brightly coloured oriental plants, flowers, birds and butterflies and the famous 'Indian tree' pattern that is still popular, cottons were often printed to imitate expensive silks and velvets that were imported from the East and from Italy.

The lightness of cotton and its washability made it very suitable for bed hangings, but bed curtains of linen embroidered with crewel work were also much in evidence. At first the crewel-work motifs were taken from pattern books and

56. The stone staircase at Drayton was built between 1702 and 1705. The superb ironwork balustrade is almost certainly by Jean Tijou while the painting of the walls, not commissioned until 1712, is by Gerard Lanscroon. This is a splendid example of illusionist painting, enhanced by the figures falling out over the plinth.

57. Cotton cloth block-printed in madder and indigo, probably dating from the late seventeenth century.

bestiaries but by the end of the seventeenth century the exotic flowers and plants in brilliant colours seen in Indian cottons were being copied. Printed cottons were also used for wall hangings and took the place of the 'stayned' cloths of the previous century. The instant popularity of imported printed cottons and silks resulted in a depression and even riots in the silk and linen weaving trades. Daniel Defoe in his *A Tour through the whole Island of Great Britain* lays the blame on Queen Mary: 'the Queen brought in the love of the fine East India calicoes, such as were then called Masslapatan Chints, Atlasses, and fine painted calicoes, which afterwards descended into the humours of the common people so much as to make them grievous to our trade, and ruining to our manufactures and the Poor; so that the Parliament were obliged to make two acts at several times to restrain and at last prohibit the use of them.' With the Revocation of the Edict of Nantes in 1685, Huguenot weavers fled from France to England and set up the silk-weaving industry at Spitalfields which was to produce some of the most beautiful eighteenth-century dress and furnishing fabrics. As well as bringing advanced techniques of weaving to England they also established a tradition of excellence in design that made Spitalfields silks renowned in Europe and America.

Luxurious textiles played an increasingly important part in decorative schemes during the seventeenth century and those who could afford it hung their rooms with tapestry, velvet or silk damask. Tapestry was considered especially suitable for hanging in bedrooms. The Mortlake Works, with the encouragement of Charles I and the brilliant abilities of the designer, Francis Cleyn, produced a series of tapestries [pl. 62] for the court and for rich patrons. A number of other tapestry works were started in England during the century particularly after the decline of Mortlake in the 1680s, a decline which had started during the Civil War. The most important of these were the 'Soho' tapestries produced towards the end of the century, many of them designed by John Vanderbank – in particular,

58. A late-seventeenth-century Soho chinoiserie tapestry probably designed by John Vanderbank.

59. The State Bed at Drayton was supplied in 1701 and the magnificent needlework hangings date from 1701–2. The box shape was in fashion some years earlier but the great height and the magnificent yellow taffeta bedhead are typical of the turn of the century. The Mortlake tapestries, designed by Francis Cleyn, were bought for the room.

a series of chinoiserie hangings for Queen Mary's withdrawing-room at Kensington Palace [pl. 58].

The concept of order in decoration, with furniture, materials and textiles chosen to achieve a balanced harmony, came from France. One of the ways of effecting this was to use the same textiles for the hangings, the seat furniture and the bed. If the size and consequence of the house warranted it, there would certainly be a 'bed of state' [pl. 59], which would be placed in a room in an important position at the end of the 'enfilade'. This French word describes the arrangement of the rooms of state that became usual in England in the latter part of the seventeenth century. The doors from each room to the next were placed in line to give an imposing vista from one end of the house to the other. As well as being very richly decorated, the actual bed might be in an alcove and, in grand houses, there was sometimes a low balustrade separating the bed from the rest of the room. This room would be used for entertaining royalty and important guests and would often have a small 'closet' off it which would also be highly ornamented and would be used for private conversation with privileged friends.

As in the previous century, beds were the single most important piece of furniture and, in the early seventeenth century,

60. The antechamber to the Queen's Bedroom at Ham House, which was redecorated in the last quarter of the seventeenth century. The faded paned hangings of damask and velvet were originally blue; the grained panelling is gilded, the floor is parquet and the cane-seated japanned-back stools had cushions to match the hangings.

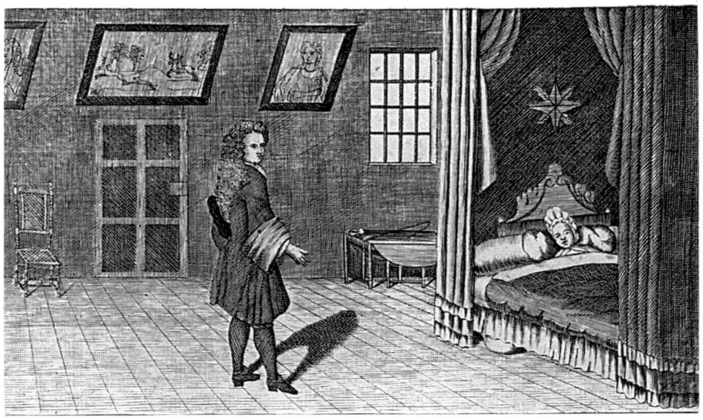

the tradition of heavily carved bed posts and headboard continued but later the bed posts were hidden by the curtains and the ornamentation of the headboard became the province of the upholsterer [pl. 61]. The upper corners of the bed would have carved finials closely covered with material to match the headboard and trimmed with fringe and tassels or a single cup shape holding plumes of feathers. With these new ideas of decoration the role of the upholsterer assumed enormous importance as he became responsible for the ever more elaborate and expensive hangings, beds and seat furniture.

The trend for chairs with cushions that were richly upholstered and heavily decorated with silver or matching fringe [pl. 65] continued during the first four decades of the century but with the Restoration, in 1660, a new form appeared. These chairs were in dark-stained wood or japanned with high backs and turned members, the backs and seats generally caned [pl. 61]. The strapwork motifs of sixteenth-century decoration were now found in textiles – for instance, in the borders of tapestries [pl. 62] or in the appliqué embroidery sometimes used, early in the century, for seat upholstery and later for elaborately decorated bedheads.

Window curtains came into common use – initially, as one piece of material hung on an iron rod by iron rings sewn onto the material itself or onto tapes. This curtain would be drawn from one side of the window but by the 1650s, we read – for instance, in the Ham House inventory of 1654 – of 'a paire' of curtains. Later, 'pull-up' curtains, which we now call festoon curtains, came to England from France – a form of curtaining that continued to be popular until the end of the eighteenth century [pl. 98].

Many different materials were used both for wall hangings and for upholstery. Leather hangings were generally gilt, punched and painted – the gilt was made by covering the leather with foil and then painting on a yellow varnish. Richly patterned leather hangings were popular throughout the century and most big houses with any pretensions to fashion would have had at least one room hung in this way. A huge variety of textiles was available – cottons, woollen materials, both plain and self-patterned, silk damasks, velvets, brocatelles [pl. 63] and many others. However, whatever the fabric, the pattern, if there was one, would be large and frequently self- coloured as in damasks. Nearly all these textiles were woven in a narrow

61. Drawing of an English bedchamber on a songsheet, *c.*1685. The bedhead is elaborately carved although the room itself is simple; the gateleg table would be used for meals taken in the bedroom. Note the canted pictures and the caned chair.

62. A Mortlake tapestry, 'Neptune and Cupid', designed and woven for Charles I – the elaborate border, typical of the work of Francis Cleyn, contains the royal cipher. (Victoria and Albert Museum, London.)

63. Two typical furnishing textiles, the red is mid- and the green late-seventeenth-century. They are both brocatelle, a mixture of linen and silk much used for hangings. Although the repeats are very long the width is only 21 inches (53 cm). The pomegranate motif had been popular since the Middle Ages.

width – about 21 inches (0.53m) – which gave plenty of scope to the upholsterer when he came to fit the hanging to the room. Also very practical in this respect was the fashion for 'paned' or panelled hangings [pl. 60]. The main fabric was divided by narrow borders, repeated at top and bottom, of matching or contrasting or toning fabric. Most grand hangings were also outlined with either fringe or passementerie of some kind.

The fashion for unified decoration, especially with regard to upholstery, was illustrated by the engravings of one particular designer – the architect Daniel Marot [pl. 67]. Marot was a Huguenot born in France in 1663, but spent his working life in Holland. After the accession of William and Mary he came to England where he styled himself *Architecte de roy de la Grande Bretagne*. He was one of the first designers working in England to produce unified schemes of decoration. Marot's designs, particularly those for beds, were extremely influential [pls. 65, 67].

After dark the only sources of light were the fire and candles and much seventeenth-century decoration was undoubtedly designed to make the most of the effect of flickering light on gilding, silver and mirrors. Most chandeliers at this time were of carved and painted or gilded wood although occasionally some were of uncut crystal or even silver, also used for wall sconces. Mirrors played an important part in decoration and in 1663, when the Duke of Buckingham established a factory at Vauxhall, mirror glass became more available; but only in small sizes and it was not until cast glass was introduced in 1773 that large plates were attainable. Rectangular mirrors in dark-coloured frames of stained pear wood, tortoiseshell, lacquer or coromandel often formed part of a triad or triolet as it is sometimes called – this arrangement consisted of a pair of candle stands to hold candelabra and a matching table, and was generally placed between the windows with a mirror in a matching frame hung above the table to reflect the light from the candles [pl. 66]. Mirrors and pictures were hung canted forward – achieved by attaching the cord at a low point on

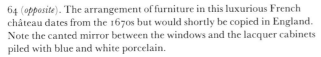

64 (*opposite*). The arrangement of furniture in this luxurious French château dates from the 1670s but would shortly be copied in England. Note the canted mirror between the windows and the lacquer cabinets piled with blue and white porcelain.

65 (*above*). The Dyrham State Bed was made for the house about 1704. Covered with crimson and yellow velvet it follows closely the designs of Daniel Marot, who often showed the rail for the case curtains in his engravings. The walnut chairs of *c.*1680 have covers to match the bed.

66. Triolet, *c.*1672, at Ham House consisting of a table and candle stands of carved ebonized pine with caned tops, and a matching ebonized pier glass.

the frame – to reflect the light, even more effectively [pl. 64].

The scale of Baroque rooms demanded important furniture and by the second half of the 1600s they were plentifully furnished compared with those of the previous century. Furniture such as beds, cabinets and even chairs increased in height to suit the height of these rooms. The East India Company brought lacquer and coromandel from the east, generally in the form of screens but sometimes already made up into cabinets which were then mounted on ornate gilded or silvered stands with aprons and sometimes with cresting to lend added height. Cabinets in other exotic materials such as tortoiseshell

67. A design for a bedroom by Daniel Marot of about 1690. The extremely elaborate flying tester bed is sitting on a bed carpet; the scalloped tops of the paned hangings and the skirts of the chairs echo the hangings of the bed. (Victoria and Albert Museum, London.)

and oyster veneer were also important elements in the overall schemes of decoration. Lacquer, in all its forms, found immediate popularity [pl. 64] – so much so that, in 1688, a *Treatise on Japanning and Varnishing* was published by John Stalker and George Parker. This book set out to describe how to imitate oriental lacquer and included suitable designs to copy. Japanning, as this imitation lacquer was called, soon became a rage, even as a pastime for ladies, and many pieces of furniture and small objects such as boxes were decorated in this way.

Marot's engravings show a variety of ways to display collections of blue and white oriental porcelain and Dutch and English Delft. Chinese blue and white porcelain had been brought, firstly, to Holland by the Dutch East India Company but it quickly became prized all over Europe. Queen Mary herself was an avid collector and Defoe also has something to say on this score: 'The Queen brought in the custom or humour, as I may call it, of furnishing houses with China Ware, which increased to a strange degree afterwards, piling their

68. Daniel Marot's design for a china room, *c.*1700. Although a number of China rooms or closets existed in England at the time none has survived in its original form. To the left of the fireplace there appears to be a lacquer panel (see pl. 52). (Victoria and Albert Museum, London.)

china upon the tops of cabinets, scrutoires and every chimney piece to the tops of ceilings, and even setting up shelves for their china ware where they wanted such places, till it became a grievance in the expense of it and even injurious to their families and estates' [pl. 68]. Large blue and white porcelain or Delft pieces, including pyramid-shaped tulip vases designed to show off single blooms, were also displayed in fireplaces during the summer.

After the death of Queen Anne in 1714 and with the arrival of the Hanoverian dynasty, the Baroque style became associated with the Jacobites, with absolutism and all the royal pretensions that had been swept away by the 'Bloodless Revolution' of 1688. In reality, English Baroque had only come to full flowering after 1688, but this fact was conveniently ignored. The new style, based on the work of Inigo Jones, was to have full political approval. Notwithstanding, certain aspects of the Baroque style persisted for a number of years – despite its unfortunate connotations!

4

THE RULE OF TASTE

In 1714 dynastic and political changes occurred that were to have a considerable effect on the visual arts. With the death of the last Stuart monarch, Queen Anne, and accession of her Hanoverian cousin, George I, the real centre of power and patronage began to shift from the court to the rich and educated landowners backed by the mercantile class, the vast majority of whom supported the Whig party. The political ascendancy of the Whigs was to last for forty-six years and produced an unprecedented 'Rule of Taste' in the arts.

In that same year three men who were to be instrumental in the introduction of these rules were in Rome suitably celebrating, one hopes, the centenary of Inigo Jones's presence there. Jones was to provide Lord Burlington, Thomas Coke and William Kent with a national focus in what was to be a 'national' taste – a taste that was to be governed by rules of reason and order applied to the arts and enforced by a Whig hierarchy. The correctness of classical architecture was to become the discipline that formed 'correct taste'. Fortunately, the chauvinistic attitude that derided everything to do with the Stuarts, Catholicism, Rome and the Baroque was conveniently overlooked when it came to travel. Thomas Coke spent another four years on the Continent and Lord Burlington paid a second visit in 1719 specifically to study the buildings of Palladio. When he returned to England he brought the painter, architect and designer William Kent with him, as well as all Palladio's drawings of Roman antiquity.

While these three were in Italy others were already busy at home paving the way for the Palladian revival. In 1710 Wilbury House in Wiltshire was 'invented and built . . . in the style of Inigo Jones' by William Benson. Wilbury was the precursor in scale of all the 'Palladian' villas that were to follow. Five years later Colen Campbell designed the first great Palladian revival house at Wanstead in Essex. Campbell included both these houses, together with buildings by Jones and his assistant, the architect John Webb, in the first volume of *Vitruvius Britannicus*, which he published in 1715, a few months before the first English edition of Palladio's *Four Books of Architecture* appeared in a translation by Giacomo Leoni. These two books effectively launched the Palladian revival. It needed only the return of Burlington, Coke and Kent to provide the

69. The gallery designed by William Kent and Lord Burlington for Burlington's villa at Chiswick, *c.*1726. The use of white and gold here provided a cool contrast to the rich wall coverings of two of the adjacent rooms. Inigo Jones's design (pl. 41) is a ghostly premonition of this gallery.

proselytizing zeal to establish the Rule of Taste, which was to impose a strictly controlled architectural framework on the decoration of houses [pl. 69].

Lord Burlington established what amounted to a private academy at Burlington House. His 'neo-Palladians' included Campbell until he was ousted by Kent, who lived there until he died, and Henry Flitcroft, who with Kent produced *Designs of Inigo Jones* under their patron's aegis in 1727. Already by the early 1720s Burlington had acquired a large number of drawings by Inigo Jones, together with his Roman sketchbook, which contained Jones's comments (quoted on p. 42) on the contrasting treatment of the exteriors and interiors of buildings. These comments from the most revered of Palladian sources liberated William Kent from the constraints implicit in the Rule of Taste when he was designing interiors [pl. 70] and, more particularly, furniture. The great Baroque tables and seats that he designed, in contrast to the ubiquitous well-mannered walnut furniture of the period, blended perfectly with the decoration of his state rooms and, indeed, of Jones's and Webb's interiors of a hundred years earlier. It would be hard to imagine a more felicitous addition to the Double Cube room at Wilton [pl. 44] than that of Kent's furniture. Twenty-five years earlier, Marot had brought upholstered furniture within the whole decorative scheme. Kent advanced the process to include benches, tables and mirrors as well.

Kent's furniture was not the only Baroque element in early neo-Palladian interiors. Plasterwork was once again in the ascendant and displayed Baroque characteristics. Just

70. The saloon at Houghton, *c.*1730, decorated by William Kent. 164 yards (148m) of crimson caffoy, costing 14s. 6d. a yard were supplied for the saloon. The magnificent Baroque seat furniture was designed by Kent almost certainly to accommodate the large pattern of the caffoy.

71. William Hogarth's family group painted in 1730–1 shows an interior that is still essentially Baroque – the crested lacquer cabinet, silver chandelier and the two-tone green hangings with a huge pattern would not be out of place in the previous century but the simple panelling of the shutters and plain buff colour are in fashion.

as the plasterers had complained of loss of livelihood, by 1715 the artists who specialized in covering walls and ceilings with illusionist painting were out of work, as the Swiss stuccatori replaced the French painters. The painted Baroque figures whose foreshortened limbs were formerly draped over painted cornices were now sculpted in stucco and draped over solid cornices [pl. 74].

From 1709 when Giovanni Bagutti arrived in London a succession of other stuccatori followed him from the vicinity of Lugano on the Swiss-Italian border. Together with Bagutti, assorted Giuseppis and Francescos of the Artari, Serena, Cortese and Vassalli families cornered the market in plasterwork for some thirty years. Their only serious English competitor was Isaac Mansfield, who worked on a number of Baroque churches for Sir Christopher Wren, Thomas Archer and James Gibbs. He was also employed by Sir John Vanbrugh and Nicholas Hawksmoor at Blenheim Palace and Castle Howard, where he assisted Bagutti. For a number of years Giuseppe Artari also worked with Bagutti so that between them the two Swiss and one native stuccatori worked for all the great English Baroque architects. It is not surprising that the early Palladians – Campbell and Leoni, Burlington and Kent – turned to these three to add Baroque flourishes of plasterwork to their otherwise strictly architectural rooms [pl. 74].

Apart from the panels on the external walls of Henry VIII's Nonsuch Palace, stucco had been unknown in England until the early eighteenth century when the Swiss stuccatori reintroduced it. In the intervening period the coarser plaster, strengthened with animal hair, had been used. The substitution of marble dust for chopped hair gave stucco its finer finish and provided the artist/craftsman with a material with which he could work in deeply sculptured relief [pl. 72]. Sculptured figures were probably modelled in situ, whereas repetitive elements such as egg and dart ornament and even vases and portrait medallions of worthies were cast from moulds and then fixed in place. As with the sixteenth- and seventeenth-century plasterwork, stucco decoration seems most usually to have been painted white on a white ground. It would seem more than probable that two distinct tones of white would have been used. Certainly colour was used in some instances before 1760, but to obtain any reliable guide to the appearance of these rooms far more scientific research is needed to establish not only the colours that were used, but the various surfaces on which they were applied.

Although the opportunities for painters were certainly

72. Staircase at Mawley Hall, *c.*1730. Italian stuccatori carried out the elaborate plasterwork with its Baroque flourishes. Both the rippling handrail which ends in a serpent's head and the setting of the balusters on a scalloped plinth are unique features. The stone floor with black insets is the most common pattern for eighteenth-century halls.

diminishing, their services had by no means been dispensed with. Their work was, however, confined within frames or panels, even if sometimes they had to simulate the frames in paint themselves. In other instances the Baroque curves of stucco work provided the frame. In the increasingly rare cases where illusionist painting was used the walls and the ceiling were treated individually. William Kent's painted arcade is confined to the walls of the King's Staircase at Kensington Palace while the dome in false perspective occupies the large central panel of the ceiling.

Inigo Jones's compartmented ceilings and coves inevitably made their reappearance at this time and were not confined to the great houses. Francis Hayman, who painted the compartments and the cove of the ceiling of the staircase at Little Haugh [pl. 73], was evidently anxious to save his client unnecessary expense when he wrote 'if you please to let the House painter prime the Ceiling &c: twice, in light Stone colour which will save me a day or two'.

For the ceiling and cove of the Presence Chamber at Kensington Palace, Kent also reintroduced the grotesque decoration that Jones and Webb had used a hundred years before at Wilton, but his use of painted and gilded 'mosaic' as a background for scrolls, animals and figures in monotone was his own invention. Although his painting of classical subjects has been understandably derided his purely decorative painting ensured his success and his position as the first great English decorator.

Below his ceilings Kent brought the walls of rooms into a Palladian context, the dominant feature of which was the fireplace. The two-tier design with its elaborate and pedimented picture frame above an equally elaborate mantelpiece [pl. 77] was known to him through Jones's and Webb's drawings, which they, in turn, had developed from French designers like Jean Barbet. There was considerable variation in the many designs Kent produced but, however different the details, they conformed to the overriding architectural concept. The two-tier design was by no means always used – the relative unimportance of a particular room or the positioning of a full-length portrait over a fireplace might determine the abandonment of the upper tier.

Kent fireplaces of both kinds found their way into houses of even quite modest size all over the country through the pattern books which had begun to appear in quantity by 1740. These cheap publications by men such as Batty Langley and William Halfpenny, were used by builders and craftsmen and the owners of houses who could not afford the services of an architect, let alone a William Kent. They provided an excellent crib and ensured the spread of the Rule of Taste.

These pattern books gave designs for staircases, panelling, doors and windows as well as fireplaces and those details favoured by Kent and others such as the Vitruvian scroll and the Greek key pattern. The designs, generally adapted from examples in great houses, often in the less important rooms, were eminently suitable for the principal rooms of manor houses, rectories and the houses of a rapidly expanding middle class. In all such houses as well as their counterparts in Scotland, Ireland and the American colonies, the patterns were followed, if sometimes with local or idiosyncratic variations.

Around 1715 bolection moulding was dropped but the recently introduced raised and fielded panels [pl. 50] were retained. This simpler version was invariably in pine painted

73. Little Haugh. The carving round the niche, over the doors and in the string of the staircase may have been added (to Palladian woodwork of 1730) when the Rococo artist, Francis Hayman, painted the ceiling in 1741. This sophisticated decoration is in a comparatively modest house.

74. The hall at Clandon, *c.*1728, with neo-Palladian architectural decoration on the walls and Baroque plasterwork probably by Giuseppe Artari on the ceiling. The legs of the stucco figures dangle over the plaster cornice like those in Baroque painted rooms (see pl. 56).

in a neutral uniform colour such as stone, grey, buff or olive green to conceal the coarse grain of the cheaper wood. The degree of the enrichment of the details of panelling, door cases and fireplaces was inevitably a matter of cost and varied enormously depending on the relative importance of both the house and the room. At the top end of the scale elaborately carved mouldings were further enhanced by gilding and in rare cases the Baroque practice of inlaying panelling with different coloured woods was revived. Paintwork was not necessarily the white enriched with gilding that we tend to associate with neo-Palladian interiors. For instance, the diarist Mrs Lybbe Powys, visiting Houghton in 1756, wrote 'the fitting up and furniture very superb; and the cornishes and mouldings of all apartments being gilt, it makes the whole what I call magnificently glaringly, more especially as the rooms are, instead of white, painted dark olive green; but this most likely will soon be altered.'

Increasingly, in the larger houses the panelling above dado level was omitted altogether, its place being taken by textiles or paper. The cut velvet and damask or the flock wallpaper which was hung on the walls was no longer broken up by 'paning' as it had been in the seventeenth century. Paning and panelling, with a strong vertical emphasis, did not make a suitable background for the pictures that were being acquired by young Englishmen on the Grand Tour which, by the eighteenth century had become a part of a young man's education. Every gentleman who could afford to do so bought objects, pictures and, in many cases, sculpture, and nearly all 'country house' collections were started in this way. When these trophies arrived back in England they had to be arranged in a suitable manner – schemes were devised to display classical busts [pl. 75] and sculpture, and special rooms were designed or set aside for pictures, such as the 'Landscape Room' at Holkham, the 'Cabinet' at Felbrigg or the dining-room at Farnborough Hall.

However, not all purchases were important enough to warrant such specialist treatment, in which case the pictures would be disposed round the walls of the saloon, having first been framed in carved and gilded wood. Many of these works were copies as it was considered infinitely preferable to own a good copy of a great picture than an inferior 'original'. If a picture was hung on a wall covered with an expensive silk or paper it was quite usual to economize by leaving the space behind blank. A great deal of trouble was taken to arrange pictures

75. The decoration of the hall at Farnborough Hall was designed to display the owner's Grand Tour purchases. The pediment over the two-tier fireplace was broken to house one of the marble busts. The flat compartments of the ceiling are repeated in the design of the stone floor.

in a proper manner, and schemes, almost invariably symmetrical, were carefully worked out – often with sketches.

Mirrors as well as pictures were now hung flat against the wall. Chairs continued to be ranged round the walls when not in use. However, there were other changes in the arrangement of furniture – the triad was replaced, between the windows, by a looking glass, no longer canted, called a pier glass. Under this was placed a table or a commode [pl. 96]. This arrangement became the rule and lasted into the early years of the nineteenth century.

At the end of the seventeenth century 'landscape' mirrors began to be placed in the panelling over chimney-pieces. These mirrors were long and low, stretching the width of the fireplace, with the actual glass often divided into three due to the difficulty of producing large mirror plates at this time. Candles were placed in branches, sometimes called girandoles, that were attached to wall brackets or mirrors – particularly landscape – or even, occasionally, pictures. A visitor, William Farington, reports in his letter describing the opening of Norfolk House after the completion of the decoration in 1756 'the

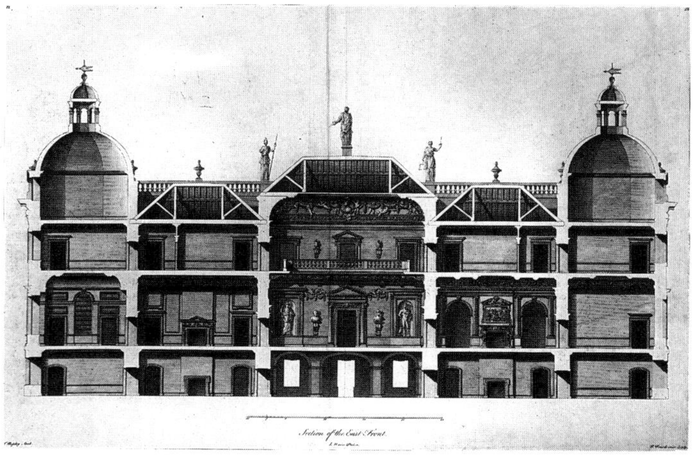

76. The section of Houghton shows the double-height hall in the centre; the great doorway leads into the saloon (pl. 70); to the right, the dining-room (pl. 77). The cuts in the wall between each room indicate the enfilade. When not entertaining the family lived on the ground floor.

next Room was Hung & Furnished with Blew-Damask, cover'd with very Fine Paintings, the Gerandoles, fix'd in the Frames of the Pictures, wch had an odd effect, & I can't think will be so good for the Paint.' Chandeliers, holding only a few candles, were still usually made of carved wood painted or gilded [pl. 70], and it was not until about the mid-eighteenth century that sliced and faceted glass drops were used to increase the reflection of light. In any case, expectations of the standard of artificial light cannot have been great as Isaac Ware in his *Complete Body of Architecture*, published in 1746, described rooms 'which if wainscoted will take six candles to light it, will in stucco require eight or if hung ten'. Wax candles were not cheap and for a grand reception at Houghton in 1730 it cost Sir Robert Walpole £15 (well over £400 at today's values) to illuminate the stone hall at Houghton with 130 wax candles and the saloon with forty.

The hall at Houghton was certainly a huge room – 40 feet (12.2m) square and 40 feet high, and identical in size and proportion to Inigo Jones's hall in the Queen's House at Greenwich. The concept of a perfect proportion for a room was taken from Palladio's own theories on the subject and was used throughout the eighteenth century. The single cube, double cube and cube and a half, formed the proportional basis for any room with pretensions to Palladian ideals and grandeur, the importance of the room being immediately established by the height which inevitably results from these principles.

These rules of architecture were accepted and understood not only by the architects but by the clients as well, and not just extremely proficient amateurs like Burlington and Coke but any self-respecting gentleman whether he had been on the Grand Tour or not. Such widespread knowledge led to an essentially architectural approach to decoration and its very formality mirrored a formal way of life and manners that had not changed from the Baroque period. The neo-Palladians did not dispense with the enfilade; if anything, they extended it – the most impressive, perhaps, being the one at Holkham which is over 330 feet (100.6m) long involving a progression through twelve rooms. Such progressions were carefully thought out in terms of their decorative and psychological effect. For instance, a suite of three rooms hung with the same textile followed by a white and gold room provided a suitable stimulus and *frisson*.

Very gradually such extremes of formality were broken down. In 1735, as Kent was finishing the decoration of Houghton, he introduced a room specifically for eating in, providing at the same time practical serving arrangements [pl. 77]. In itself no barrier to formality it nevertheless represented a new approach to planning which within fifteen years was extended to the whole house. Once all the main rooms had been planned around a central hall or staircase it was no longer thought desirable to impress visitors with endless vistas through a succession of state rooms [pl. 76]. One example of such planning was Norfolk House, where the francophile

Duchess of Norfolk gave the reception referred to earlier. To quote Farington again, 'every room was furnished with a different colour, which used to be reckon'd absurd, but this I Suppose is to be the standard' and 'the next Room is large, Wainscotted in a whimsical Taste, the Pannels fill'd with extreme fine Carvings, the Arts & Sciences all Gilt, as well the Ceiling, which was the same design.' The whimsical taste was the immensely fashionable Rococo and although the design of the panelling in the French Rococo style was rare in England the Rococo stuccowork of the ceiling was already a familiar sight. By this time English craftsmen had largely taken over from the Swiss stuccatori and had set up in London and various provincial centres. The immediacy of stucco had the great advantage of being able to adapt to new fashions, and its plasticity made it the perfect medium for the interpretation of the new Rococo style [pl. 78].

The Rococo came from France, and in England it was a definite reaction against the 'architectural' decoration of neo-

77. The Marble Parlour at Houghton was fitted up as a dining-room by William Kent in 1733, with practical service alcoves on either side of the two-tiered fireplace. This wall and the alcoves are lined with grey veined Carrara marble with mauve marble columns.

Palladianism. The light-hearted exuberance of this style was expressed in almost every aspect of the interior. The major characteristics of the Rococo are the flowing, sinuous line, the asymmetrical designs and the lavish use of scrolls in both S and C shapes [pls. 79, 80]. Natural forms, particularly plants and flowers, were used in designs for textiles and wallpapers many of which were interchangeable. Patterned Spitalfields silks were at the height of their popularity but such designs were not always woven – silk was also painted, imported from

78. Rococo plasterwork at Farnborough Hall, *c.*1750. The two iron hooks, originally intended to support a pier glass, have been incorporated to 'support' the rings. The plasterer was either Thomas Roberts or William Perritt, who was responsible for the rest of the room.

79. Trade card for a paperhanging warehouse, *c.*1750. This shows the familiar ingredients of Rococo design – sinuous S and C scrolls, shells, rockwork and naturalistic flowers and foliage within a framework displaying asymmetric variations.

80. The meandering line, derived from Hogarth's *Line of Beauty*, and often expressed as ribbon or lace, was a popular motif for textiles and wallpapers throughout the Rococo period. These two patterns come from a pattern book for Foster & Co. from *c.*1755-1800. (Victoria and Albert Museum, London.)

81. A rare survival of mid-eighteenth-century silk, hand painted in imitation of Spitalfields woven silks. The cushion is from the Bower, Castle Ashby, and still retains its original trimming.

China or made in England, the latter following closely designs for woven and printed materials [pl. 81]. In 1759 the Countess of Kildare ordered a 150 yards (137m) of painted taffeta for her house in Ireland, rather to the dismay of her husband to whom she writes, 'about the taffeta . . . Indeed, I own I had no sort of idea that it wou'd come to so much money, having seen beds at Woburn, Petworth and other places (not in the best apartments) of this sort . . . The quantity was what Spring told me was necessary for our two beds, a pair of window curtains, and four chairs; but since it cost so much I shall be almost tempted, if you approve to hang the Main drawing room with it, 'tis so elegant and beautiful a thing . . . since 'tis bought I must tell you I am out of my wits at the thoughts of being in possession of what I think the loveliest, sweetest thing in the world . . . And now, my Jemmy, what do you think is the difference between this and the frightful Nassau damask they sell in Dublin? You wou'd not have thought that a very unreasonable demand; well nine shillings a yard is what they

82. These remarkable needlework hangings were installed at Castle Ashby in 1772. They were worked by the aunts of the 8th Earl of Northampton in the seventeenth-century style of paned hangings with chinoiserie landscapes. The top border imitates festoon curtains with tassels such as would have protected real tapestries.

ask here for that . . . 150 yards of that comes to £67.10, and the sweet India taffeta stands us in at £70.0.0. what a vast difference in the beauty! and how little in the price! The breadth being the same, and as to India taffeta not being lasting, if anybody says it, send them to look at that at Goodwood, which has been up forty years. In short it is as cheap *silk* furniture as one can have.' As she makes plain, it was still the fashion to match window and bed curtains and the upholstery of seat furniture.

Copper-plate printing, which was introduced in the Rococo period, revolutionized the appearance of cotton textiles as it made possible a larger repeat and much finer definition. This method was used for the *toiles de Jouy* [pl. 83], which were first printed in Ireland in 1752 – it was not until 1770 that a factory was set up at Jouy in France, from whence comes the name. The designs for these monochrome textiles – usually blue, purple, red or sepia on a white ground – were derived from various

sources such as prints but also from French designers such as François Boucher and Jean Pillement, the latter providing a source for chinoiserie. However, printed cottons still often emulated silk patterns, and naturalistic designs of flowers scattered across a plain background, often interspersed with birds, went on being manufactured during the sixties and seventies. These light attractive fabrics were particularly suitable for bedrooms and were also often used for loose case covers for seat furniture, as were woven check cottons.

The most usual form of curtain was still the draw-up or festoon curtain but with the addition of heavy pelmets that were carved in flat scrolls and either covered in fabric to match the curtains or gilded. This type of carved pelmet was also used for beds, which in general ceased to have cups and plumes as finials. One of the difficulties encountered with the new neo-Palladian style was that of curtaining Venetian windows. Many of these were in fact not curtained at all and relied on shutters with which practically all windows were supplied. However, Thomas Chippendale in his *Director* shows an extremely ingenious way of using a pelmet board to overcome this problem: the carved pelmet, in the Rococo style, follows the shape of the window and from it is hung a looped swag from which the curtains drop at either side. The curvilinear shapes were very suitable for pelmets, both for windows and for beds and some highly successful examples have survived as, for instance, the amazing Rococo bed at Petworth House.

In the first half of the eighteenth century needlework again came into its own [pl. 82] and embroidered hangings were used for bed curtains. Seat furniture was also often upholstered in needlework both floral and illustrative – both *Aesop's Fables* and *Gay's Fables* were depicted by William Kent. Bed carpets were often embroidered and Mrs Delaney, a famous needlewoman, writes in 1752, 'My candlelight work is finishing a carpet in double cross-stitch, on very coarse canvas, to go round my bed.' Some of the most beautiful needlework carpets were produced at this time, most of them, as far as we know, the work of amateurs. They are basically floral in design, in natural colours on a plain ground, very little of which can be seen; some, however, have coats of arms or crests in the centre [pl. 47]. There was also a considerable increase in the use of large Turkey carpets, as can be seen in innumerable conversation pieces [pl. 84]. As in the seventeenth century, stone or marble, laid in patterns, was used for floors of halls [pl. 72], and similar patterns were sometimes painted on wooden floors. Other less geometric patterns were also used for painted floors – the most famous of those that survive being at Belton, where the centre is painted with the arms of the Tyrconnel family.

Although wallpaper had been manufactured since the sixteenth century in England it was not until the eighteenth century that it began to be used in any quantity and by 1712 a tax was levied on paper to be painted, printed or stained. Late in the seventeenth century the hitherto small pieces of paper were being pasted together to form a roll, making it possible to print patterns with a very much larger repeat;

83. Copper-plate printed *toile de Jouy* showing rustic scenes.

it also made the hanging of the paper much easier. From advertisements of the time, it seems that these papers sought to imitate other hangings such as tapestry and damask, which in due course wallpaper would replace as fashionable decoration. Flock paper was generally designed to reproduce the patterns of expensive textiles, particularly Italian silks.

Wallpaper began to be considered suitable for reception rooms around the 1730s when a flock paper with a huge repeat – just over 6½ feet (2m) in height by 1½ feet (0.5m) wide – was hung in the Whitehall offices of the Privy Council. This particular crimson flock paper, so very much cheaper than the silk it sought to emulate, was used in a large number of interiors of neo-Palladian houses. Crimson was a favourite colour for grand rooms or 'rooms of parade'. On a visit to Holkham Hall in 1756 Mrs Powys wrote, 'from this you come into a very fine saloon, hung with crimson velvet, the cornishes richly gilt . . . On one side of the saloon is a dressing room, bed-chamber, and inner apartment . . . all to be hung with and furnished

84. Painting of the Corbally family, shown in a room hung with one of the new chiaroscuro papers introduced to England in the 1750s. The family is depicted in the centre of the room (on a large Turkey carpet), but the rest of the furniture is ranged round the walls as was correct in the eighteenth century.

85. Wood-block and stencil wallpaper in an 'Indian' design in shades of blue and brown, early eighteenth century. (Victoria and Albert Museum, London.)

as the saloon; on the other side are the same rooms . . . hung and furnished with crimson damask.'

By the 1740s a wide variety of papers was being produced. English papers were exported to France as well as America; in 1754 Mme de Pompadour chose English flock paper at Versailles and Mme de Genlis, the famous educationalist, wrote that ladies 'even relegate to storage their magnificent Gobelins tapestries to put English bluepaper in their place'. In 1754 John Baptist Jackson published a book entitled *An Essay on the Invention of Engraving and Printing in Chiaro Oscuro as practise by Albert Durer, Hugo di Carpia, and the Application of it to the making of Paper Hangings of Taste, Duration and Elegance*. Jackson had worked in Paris, Rome and Venice and when he returned to London in 1746 he started manufacturing as well as designing wallpaper. In his book he explains how to fit up houses with elegance, cheapness and taste: 'By this way of printing Paper the Inventor has contrived that the Lights and Shades shall be broad and bold . . . the finest Prints of all the antique Statues . . . are introduced into niches of Chiaro Oscuro in the Pannels of their Paper . . . Thus the Person who cannot purchase the Statues themselves, may have these Prints in their Place.' He then goes on to say that if landscapes are preferred, prints taken from Salvator Rosa, Claude, Poussin and so on can be substituted.

These 'chiaro oscuro' papers [pl. 87] had a revolutionary effect on wall decoration and they continued in popularity until the end of the century. Jackson was an extremely prolific designer over a wide range of subjects and the enchanting

86. Early-eighteenth-century wool velvet wall hanging. The door architrave is a good example of enrichment of the neo-Palladian period as is the colour combination of crimson, white and gold. The fillet is missing.

papers he produced using naturalistic sprays and trails of flowers and plants were popular for many years [pl. 88]. One of his other innovations was to print in oil, but this did not prove any more satisfactory than the conventional distemper colours. From the 1750s wallpaper was printed from wood blocks and it was not until the early nineteenth century that the introduction of cylinder printing machines revolutionized production.

Hand-painted Chinese wallpapers were beginning to be

imported in the late 1600s but they were not used in any great quantity before about 1740; from then on they became extremely popular, especially for bedrooms [pl. 89] – the more so, as they combined so charmingly with the Rococo style. The paper was imported in rolls every one of which was painted with individual plants, flowers and birds or different scenes but all designed to match up to form a continuous whole. The background colours were most commonly green, blue or tobacco brown. These expensive hand-painted Chinese papers influenced English manufacturers (not, however, Jackson who disapproved of them), who produced printed papers with chinoiserie designs and also hand-painted ones in direct

imitation – a fashion that was to be revived in the early years of the twentieth century.

The taste for chinoiserie was one of the manifestations of the Rococo style and this appeared in a variety of ways – perhaps the most extreme being the decoration, all of carved wood, at Claydon House [pl. 93]. Thomas Chippendale's *The Gentleman and Cabinet-Maker's Director* was published in 1754 and advertised as *Being a New Book of Designs of Household Furniture in the Gothic, Chinese and Modern Taste*. It contained a large num-

87. A typical John Baptist Jackson 'Chiaro Oscuro' wallpaper, *c.*1769. (Victoria and Albert Museum, London.)

88. A drawing by Jackson, from an album used by the artist for his wallpaper designs. (Victoria and Albert Museum, London.)

89. Chinese wallpaper at Nostell Priory. The carved green and gold fillet which Chippendale designed and made follows the outline of the mouldings. Chinese wallpaper reflected and may have influenced the lightness of decoration in the middle of the eighteenth century. English versions were also made, sometimes using cut-out figures and birds.

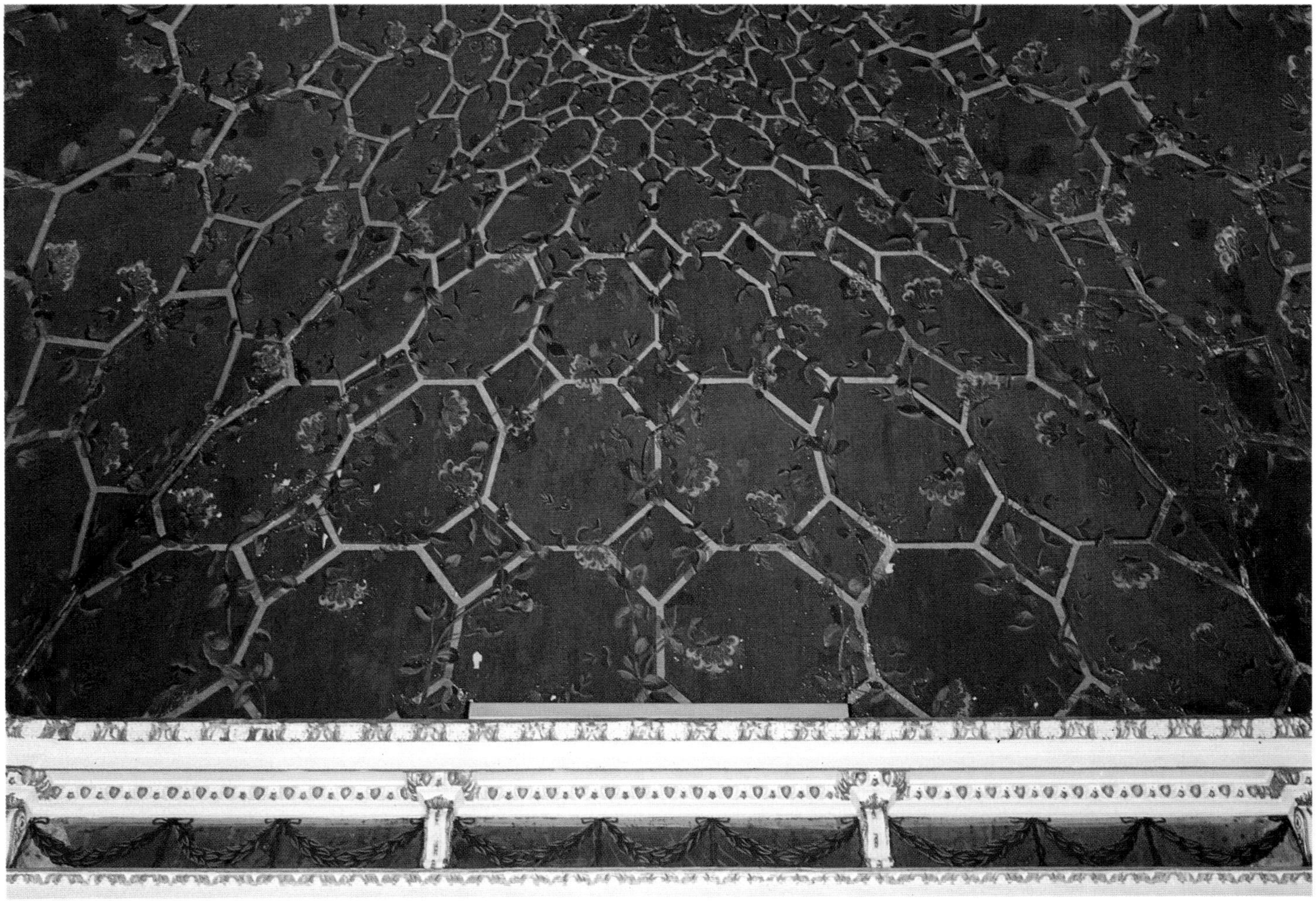

ber of designs, mostly in the Rococo or 'modern' taste. It is impossible to overestimate the importance of the *Director*, which went into two further editions and had an influence on taste out of all proportion to the number of copies produced. It was here that the designs for fantastic mirrors and chairs with 'Chinese Fret', which we know as 'Chinese Chippendale', were first seen [pl. 92]. It also included that other facet of Rococo taste – the Gothic – with illustrations of chairs, bookcases and other pieces of furniture displaying pointed and ogee arches, quatrefoils and other Gothic features in the carved ornament.

To the early eighteenth-century eye the Gothic had had no artistic merit but it did not inhibit architects from using Gothic details in a playful and decorative manner. From the 1730s Kent had been using Gothic 'gimmicks' where he thought they were appropriate and indeed the curves of ogee and quatrefoil were a gift to the Rococo designers. The most famous exponent of Rococo Gothic was Horace Walpole. His house, Strawberry Hill at Twickenham [pls. 94, 95] became so famous that he had to issue tickets to control the flow of visitors. This form of Gothic, however, was no more medieval than chinoiserie was Chinese! Both were strongly imbued with Rococo lightheartedness and a spirit of fantasy and although Horace Walpole certainly studied medieval and Tudor buildings he just took what he liked and used it in the way he wanted. As he said 'one has the satisfaction of imprinting the gloomth of abbeys and cathedrals on one's house'.

90. Detail of Andien de Clermont's *singerie* (monkey) ceiling at Narford Hall, 1739–40. Clermont's fellow countrymen Antoine Watteau and Claude Audran had painted a Singerie Room in the Château de Marly in 1709. Clermont often painted other animals and birds with his monkeys.

91. Coved ceiling in the Reading Closet at Wentworth Castle painted with honeysuckle entwined round a gilt trellis and attributed to Andien de Clermont, *c.*1745. The frieze is of mirror glass painted with swags of bay leaves. The walls below were originally hung with painted satin. The modern painting and gilding of the cornice is unfortunate.

Horace Walpole's description of a room at Strawberry Hill also gives a hint of a change of direction away from the Rococo: 'Out of this closet is the room where we always live, hung with a blue and white paper in stripes adorned with festoons, and a thousand plump chairs, couches, and luxurious settees covered with linen of the same pattern, and with a bow-window commanding the prospect and gloomed with limes that shade half of each window, already darkened with painted glass in chiaroscuro, set in deep blue glass. Under this is a cool little hall, where we generally dine, hung with paper to imitate Dutch tiles.' The spontaneity and frivolity of the Rococo was unlikely to last – it was above all else a purely fashionable style. Although its charm obviously appealed to Walpole, he and a number of other men in the middle of the eighteenth century began to pursue another course – one that was more serious, but essentially romantic in origin.

92 (*opposite*). The State Bedchamber at Nostell designed *c.*1750 by James Paine, probably as a music room. It was redecorated in 1769–70 by Thomas Chippendale who supplied the 'Indian' paper, the green lacquer furniture and the 'Chinese Chippendale' mirror (the bed is later, as are the hangings, curtains and carpet).

93 (*above*). This example of chinoiserie Rococo carving is almost as elaborate as that in the Chinese room at Claydon, though less well executed. Ho-ho birds are incorporated in the design (cf. pl. 92).

94. The Refectory, Strawberry Hill. At the time when Richard Bentley and Walpole designed the Refectory, in 1750, Walpole's taste reflected the fashionable Rococo Gothic.

95. The Holbein Chamber, Strawberry Hill, 1759, represents the beginnings of Walpole's archaeological interest in the Gothic. The design of the fireplace came partly from the high altar at Rouen and partly from a tomb in Canterbury Cathedral. Walpole bought the Indo-Portuguese chairs believing them to be Elizabethan.

5

CLASSICAL REVIVALS

During the 1750s when the Rococo fashion was at its height Englishmen began burrowing more deeply into the past. New and more extensive excavations had already begun at Herculaneum and Pompeii in the 1740s but the Grand Tourists did not confine their attentions to sites in Italy – Greece, Dalmatia and the Near East were added to their itineraries. Their studies and the books which they published as a result were informed by what might be called an archaeological approach to the subject. Horace Walpole, too, was to view medieval buildings in this way. As Sir John Summerson has pointed out, archaeology is 'fundamentally, an irrational quest for the golden age of the past, classical or medieval' and 'essentially romantic' in origin. If the quest was propelled by romanticism the result was a broader and deeper study of classical antiquity than that of the neo-Palladian, who had tended to view Roman buildings through Palladio's eyes.

The new excavations increased the vocabulary of classical ornament and as the buildings gradually became visible above the earth this ornament could be studied at eye level. This detailed study of a greatly increased number of archaeological sites by a new generation of architects and their patrons led to the establishment of neo-classicism as a fashionable style by the early 1760s [pl. 101].

It was, however, fated to be primarily a style of decoration. Few great neo-classical houses were built following the building boom of the first half of the early eighteenth century. It was no coincidence that four-fifths of the domestic work undertaken by the two greatest architects of the period, Robert Adam and William Chambers, was confined to alterations and additions. Fortunately for the owners of recently built houses the rules of proportion that had governed neo-Palladian interiors had not changed, making it relatively easy to introduce a new scheme of decoration without structural alteration.

Robert Adam and William Chambers were extremely ambitious. Both had been grounded in the neo-Palladian style before their extensive Grand Tours and both had spent time in Paris and were subject to a strong French influence most noticeably in their designs for furniture. The elder of the two, Chambers, had made several visits to China in the 1740s and

96. The saloon at Saltram by Robert Adam, who also designed the pier glasses and probably the pier tables. The seat furniture is by Thomas Chippendale and the plasterwork was executed by the firm of Joseph Rose, with painted roundels by Antonio Zucchi; the torchères are by Matthew Boulton and the carpet, to Adam's design echoing the ceiling, was woven at Axminster.

97. *Lady Friz at her Toilet*, a satirical print, *c.*1780. The festoon curtains of striped fabric are half down and the variety of pattern shown in wallpaper, carpet and flowered bed hangings is unusual. The draped toilet mirror was a popular fashion during the second half of the eighteenth century.

in 1757 published his *Designs of Chinese Buildings* in which he illustrated authentic Chinese buildings, interiors and furniture, at the precise time his fellow countrymen were indulging in the purely fanciful Rococo chinoiserie and on whom Chambers's book made not the slightest impression. It nevertheless was one more example of the preoccupation of the 1750s of recording and publishing material from the original source.

Successively tutor to George, Prince of Wales, and then his architect when he became king, William Chambers was finally able to drop his private clients and concentrate for the last twenty-odd years of his life on his masterpiece – the vast complex of public offices at Somerset House. In general, the interiors of his houses display a more selective and fastidious use of neo-classical ornament than those of Robert Adam [pl. 100]. Ultimately one senses the architect is in charge rather than the decorator [pl. 99], which is perhaps the reason why he did not have the fashionable success of his rival Adam. The reaction against the powerful architectural decoration of neo-Palladian interiors that had resulted in the purely decorative schemes of the Rococo designers did not disappear with Adam, who placed so much emphasis on decoration. The charming even feminine qualities of the Rococo and of Adam's neo-classical rooms provide a distinct contrast to those of Burlington's and Coke's time, when every cultivated man was presumed to be his own architect.

When Robert Adam landed at Harwich in January 1758 after a Grand Tour that had lasted for four years he was determined to become the leading figure in the field of architecture and decoration. We have seen that circumstances largely thwarted his architectural ambitions but his success as a decorator was immediately assured. Within twelve years he had carried out the vast majority of his most important commissions, almost all of which involved the redecoration of existing houses, although in many cases this entailed extensive and

98. Mrs Congreve and her daughters in their London drawing-room, 1782. The festoon curtains are drawn up and the pictures and mirrors with candle branches are fashionably arranged in pairs. The splendid carpet could be Axminster. (National Gallery of Ireland, Dublin.)

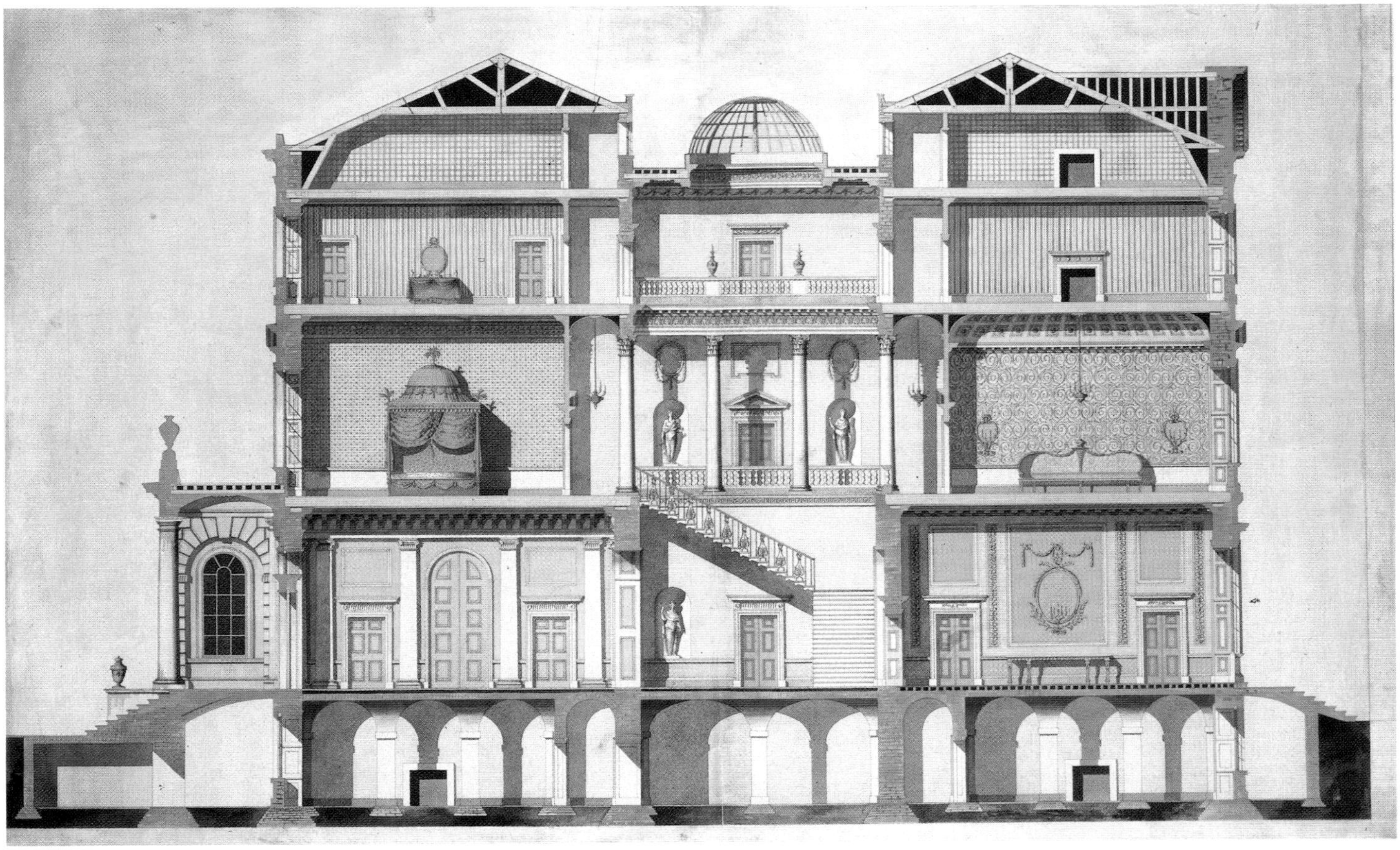

large-scale alterations and additions. In some instances he took over from other architects before the house, invariably a late neo-Palladian one, was finished and where, one hopes, John Carr, Lancelot Brown and James Paine gave way with a good grace.

Robert Adam's father had been the most successful neo-Palladian architect in Scotland and Robert himself was certainly influenced by William Kent's work, but this did not inhibit him in changing the whole emphasis in his interiors from the architectural to the decorative. In the same way that the elaborate architectural details of neo-Palladian exteriors were simplified or omitted altogether from the facades of his neo-classical houses, so prominent architectural features no longer dominated his interiors. Door-cases, fireplaces and ceilings were integrated much more closely within the whole decorative scheme. The upper tier of the fireplace was dispensed with altogether and the strong structural appearance of

99 (*top*). Section of a house drawn in 1774 by John Yenn, a pupil and disciple of Sir William Chambers. Yenn followed Chambers in showing a decorative scheme for a house in this way. The grouping of rooms round a central staircase was an innovation that had been used by a number of architects. Note the lyre-shaped cast-iron balusters which Adam had first introduced.

100 (*left*). Detail of a bedroom at Osterley designed by Sir William Chambers. The neo-classical garland of husks appears to emerge from a background of Rococo ribbons, shells and C scrolls surmounting the frame of the Chinese glass painting. This dates from the late 1750s – the period when neo-classicism began to take over from Rococo.

the neo-Palladian ceiling was replaced by one displaying only decorative qualities. The compartments formerly defined by deep beams were now outlined only by flat borders carrying more decoration. Elaborately ornamented compartments were not confined to ceilings, they were used extensively on walls, as pilasters on door-cases, and even as panels on fireplaces.

Adam used a great variety of classical motifs such as palmettes, anthemions or honeysuckle flowers, husks, bucrania or ox skulls, sphinxes and groups of figures in classical dress and poses. These latter were often enclosed in round, oval or rectangular shapes. This new decoration was applied to furniture as well as walls, where it was expressed in paint or plasterwork [pl. 104]. The smaller motifs were often cast in papier mâché or composition, and were not always well received. The sculptor John Flaxman lamented of his plaques, designed for chimney-pieces: 'I know they are much cheaper at that price than marble, and every way better, but people will not compare things which they conceive to be made out of moulds, or perhaps stamped at a blow like the Birmingham articles, with carving in natural stones where they are certain no moulding, casting, or stamping can be done.'

Architects working in the second half of the eighteenth century were particularly well served by the artists and craftsmen who interpreted their designs. Artists such as Giovanni Battista Cipriani, Francisco Zuccarelli, Angelica Kauffmann and Antonio Zucchi, who had worked for Robert Adam in Italy, were available to paint charming vignettes to adorn the walls and ceilings of houses such as Buckingham Palace, Kenwood, Syon and Osterley. The restrained and delicate plasterwork in very elaborate patterns was interpreted by firms

101. The hall at Purbrook House designed by Sir Robert Taylor in 1770 was probably the first re-creation in England of a Roman atrium the gallery of which serves the bedrooms. The restrained neo-classical plasterwork is dominated by the architectural decoration. (Painting by Thomas Malton, Ashmolean Museum, Oxford.)

102. The Marble Hall at Kedleston, designed by Robert Adam in the early 1760s. The idea of this great Roman atrium probably originated with James Paine but the decoration is Adam's. The 25-foot-high (7.6 m) columns of alabaster are relieved by the lightness of Joseph Rose's plasterwork. The hall retains the original colours.

88
The back of Chairs for the first room
is the same pattern as this, but has a yellow
ground as that of the bottom,
in the original drawing the white & red husks were kept more apart
Adelphi
30. Decr. 1778 –
SOANE 88 MUSEUM
Back of Chairs for the
second Room at Sir A: Hume
in Hill Street
Adelphi

such as that of Joseph Rose, which had been in existence since the early 1750s. In the 1760s Joseph Rose took his nephew and namesake into partnership. The younger Rose had spent some years in Italy studying classical remains, preparing himself as the ideal craftsman to carry out Robert Adam's designs. Indeed, the firm of Joseph Rose was responsible for the plasterwork in nearly all Adam's great commissions [pl. 102].

The change from Rococo to neo-classical plasterwork was not only in the different motifs but also in the handling of the plaster – the tendency now was for a much flatter look with less and less relief, and instead of swirling, asymmetrical scrolls and curves the patterns of delicate arabesques, paterae, drops of husks and fragile-looking garlands were arranged in rhythmic compositions. One of the decorative innovations of the neo-classical period was in the colouring of the plasterwork. In general, up to this date plasterwork had been either all white or the motifs had been white on a coloured ground. Now colours were mixed and different compartments on ceilings and walls were painted in colours that matched only in tone, while the plasterwork itself was picked out and sometimes gilded. The entire surface of ceilings was decorated, either coffered or compartmented, and each coffer or compartment would be filled by a motif or figure painted on canvas or by plasterwork [pls. 105, 106].

103. A design by Robert Adam for the upholstery for a chair back, *c.*1778. (Sir John Soane's Museum, London.)

104. Robert Adam's design for the rear parlour at 10 Portman Square, *c.*1775, showing his use of pilasters as a vehicle for decoration and the delicate small-scale neo-classical detail. (Sir John Soane's Museum, London.)

It is revealing that when, in 1775, Lady Sarah Bunbury was advising her sister about the decoration of a small house in Ireland her major recommendations for walls and ceilings were for decorative painting and painted plasterwork. She adds, 'you may grow tired of a fancy finishing; so be very sure you will like it for ten or fifteen years at least; for by that time it will be dirty and old fashioned'. Where she indicates textile hangings she suggests French grey, green or white damask, satin, Indian taffeta or lutestring. These colours are typically much lighter than those admired and used earlier in the century, perhaps as a result of the clear, light tones used by Adam, Chambers and other designers for plasterwork. Where the predominant colour for room schemes in the second quarter of the eighteenth century seems to have been blue, this now changes to pea green [pl. 108] – a colour that is constantly referred to and that is used for decoration of every kind.

105. Ceiling design of 1768 by Robert Adam for the Breakfast room, Kedleston. Maidens hold back the garlands which are painted with scrolls of foliage (*rinceau*).

106. The saloon at Brocket Hall was designed by James Paine *c.* 1772. This large room, 58 feet (17 m) long, is hung with 'exceeding rich flowered (crimson) damask' and the curtain drapery under the arched pelmets is original. The ceiling compartments painted by Mortimer and Heatley were not finished until 1784.

The neo-classical architects were the first to design complete schemes for interiors and, in the case of Robert Adam, no detail was too small to merit his attention. He designed the decoration of the walls and ceiling, often the furniture and even its upholstery [pl. 103], the carpet, the fire grate and the door furniture as well as the light fittings and pelmets for the curtains [pl. 109]. He also did not hesitate to tell his clients how to use the rooms he designed; for instance, when Lord Shelburne bought the house Adam was building for Lord Bute (it then became Shelburne and later Lansdowne House) he explained that the ante-room, which was the first in the suite of levee rooms, was for receiving visitors. This led on to the room for company before dinner and then on into the eating room (which had plasterwork by Joseph Rose and niches for statues). After dinner the guests were expected to pass into the centre of the house, the staircase hall, and across to the north-east drawing-room!

Robert Adam was not the first architect to design floors to echo the ceiling but he used this idea to very great effect in many of the important houses in which he worked. He nearly always subtly varied the floor from the exact pattern of the ceiling, whether using stone, marble, or scagliola. He also followed this scheme for carpets, for which he produced designs for at least twenty-three different houses. Fortunately, he was able to call upon the services of both the Moorfields and the Axminster manufactories of hand-knotted carpets to execute these designs. From the early 1760s until the end of the century these were the only two manufacturers producing knotted carpets in England. Although they worked for Adam and other architects in the neo-classical style, they also produced carpets in the Turkish style and patterns using flowers and garlands still echoing the Rococo. In less grand houses Turkey carpets were still very much in evidence in the more important rooms, but by the 1760s it was considered fashionable to have fitted carpets of either Brussels or Wilton.

The first carpet workshop for weaving Brussels and flat car-

107. In this late-eighteenth-century conversation piece the lady at her netting is sitting on a chair with a case cover. Note also the classical figure and gryphon candlesticks on the mantelshelf, the Greek key pattern dado rail, the tassel on the curtain pull, and the all-over-patterned fitted carpet.

108. This painting by George Morland, typical of his rather sentimental pictures of the 1780s, shows a one-colour decorative scheme. The rather Rococo wallpaper is offset by the more fashionable striped silk used for the curtains and the cover of the painted chair.

peting seems to have been set up at Kidderminster as early as 1735 and those at Wilton shortly after, in 1740. These carpets were woven in narrow strips with repeating patterns so that they could be fitted wall to wall [pls. 107, 110]. They could be easily cut to fit around fireplaces and could be provided with decorative borders. They also had the advantage of being immeasurably cheaper than 'bespoke' or oriental carpets. In 1756 Isaac Ware wrote, 'The use of carpeting at this time has set aside the ornamenting of floors in a great measure; it is the custom almost universally to cover a room entirely; so that there is no necessity of any beauty or workmanship underneath.'

Floor cloths had been introduced in the early years of the eighteenth century; they consisted of canvas treated with size and then covered with a good many coats of paint to give a smooth, hard-wearing finish that could be plain or patterned. Geometric chequer patterns seem to have been popular to begin with [pl. 31] and by the 1760s designs imitating mosaic pavements were in fashion, in keeping with the neo-classical style. Floor cloths in patterns following the prevailing fashions were laid in many parts of the house, even in grand entrance halls – for instance, at Attingham in 1827 there was 'a handsome square piece of stone and slate colour octagon panelled roset-pattern Floor-cloth'. Their traditional use continued in parts of the house which would receive heavy wear or was liable to spillage – under sideboards, where they were patterned to match the carpet, and under washstands. It was eventually replaced by linoleum, which was patented in 1860. Fabric crumb cloths were sometimes put down when the dining table was set up and then removed. These continued in use until 1914.

The 'hardware' designed by architects such as James 'Athenian' Stuart, William Chambers, James Wyatt and Robert Adam was manufactured with superb craftsmanship by firms such as that of Matthew Boulton. Boulton was a hardware manufacturer whose factory just outside Birmingham produced items of outstanding quality in Sheffield plate, ormolu and other metals. As well as manufacturing the door furniture, candelabra, wall sconces, and fire furniture to order for commissions by architects, Boulton offered for sale articles designed by Adam, Chambers and Wyatt and work from his own team of designers. He was particularly successful in the mounting of Bluejohn in ormolu, much of which was exported to France (from where this Derbyshire fluorspar gets its name '*bleu-jaune*'). The first large deposit was not mined until 1743 but it immediately became extremely popular and was used for candelabra and also for urns and vases elaborately mounted in ormolu for chimney 'garnitures'.

The idea of using the chimney shelf for the display of objects seems to have been introduced to England when designs for chimney-pieces began to be based on classical proportions. As vases and statues were used on the skyline of Renaissance buildings so it seemed logical to place a variety of different-shaped objects and vases on the shelf of an 'architectural' chimney-piece and they are often shown in drawings of designs for fire-

109. Designs for a fireplace, pelmets and torchères from *The Works in Architecture of Robert and James Adam*, issued as a single volume in 1778.

110. A young Englishman at breakfast, *c.*1780. The dropleaf table would have been set up for this informal meal and the chairs still have their red and white check case covers. The pattern of the fitted carpet and border derives from Roman tesselated pavements. The plain fabric or wallpaper has a gilded fillet. (Painting attributed to Henry Walton, Toledo Museum of Art, Ohio.)

111. The Etruscan Dressing-Room at Osterley House was designed by Robert Adam when he altered the Jacobean house for the rich banker Mr Child. The cane-seated chairs were designed by Adam in 1776 and painted to correspond with the decoration of the walls. The firescreen, was worked by Mrs Child to a design by Adam, who also designed the chimney board, although it is not seen in use here.

112. The antechamber or Tapestry Room at Osterley Park is hung with French Gobelins tapestry ordered in 1772. The tapestry depicts the elements, with *trompe-l'œil* medallion paintings by François Boucher. The matching chairs were designed by Linnel and the carpet was woven by Moore. The plasterwork ceiling was designed by Robert Adam in 1772.

113. These pelmets were made in Chippendale's workshops and are of carved wood which imitates heavy taffeta. They were the only window 'curtains' intended for the Gallery at Harewood House with decoration designed by Robert Adam in 1769.

places [pl. 109]. Chinese porcelain, arriving with the East India Company, was enormously popular for 'suites of chimney ornaments' throughout the late 1600s and right up to the 1760s. These suites were in sets of unequal number and generally consisted of pairs of different-shaped vases and beakers with a single one for the centre. In the second half of the eighteenth century English factories such as Lowestoft and Worcester made 'garnitures', often in the Chinese taste. Large vases and urns, sometimes filled with flowers, were still often placed in fireplaces in the summertime. Alternatively a chimney board, painted to simulate the vase of flowers or the grate or just decorated en suite with the room, was fitted into the fireplace opening to shut off draughts. Robert Adam's design for the chimney board for the Etruscan Dressing-Room at Osterley is recorded in the 1782 inventory: 'The Room hung with Canvas and Paper and very elegantly painted with Etruscan ornaments and Chimney board ditto' [pl. 111].

114. Design for a neo-classical pier glass and table and alternative pelmets, by the cabinet-maker John Linnel (1723-99). (Victoria and Albert Museum, London.)

When neo-classical ornament became fashionable many 'suites of chimney ornaments' in the shape of vases were replaced by figures, obelisks and candelabra in the classical taste that were more in keeping with the new style of chimney-piece. It was at this time that Josiah Wedgwood perfected his 'Black Basaltes'. This very fine, hard, black stoneware was ideally suited for busts and vases, as it could bear fine ornament and it could also be 'bronzed'. Wedgwood also made bough pots and what he called dressing flower pots for use with fresh flowers. In 1772 he wrote, 'Vases are furniture for a Chimney piece – Bough pots for a hearth, under a slab or Marble Table; I think they never can be used one instead of the other.'

The role of the upholsterer became increasingly important but his functions became more various as time went on so that by the mid-eighteenth century upholsterers were not only suppliers of a large number of different goods but they were also acting as decorators. An idea of the range that could be supplied comes from a letter from Sophie von la Roche when she visited the establishment of the cabinet-maker George Seddon. After visiting all the departments for furniture, mirrors, gilding and so on, she concludes, 'Chintz, silk and wool materials for curtains and bed-covers; hangings in every possible material; carpets and stair-carpets to order; in short anything one might desire to furnish a house'. The most famous firm of this kind was that of Chippendale and Haig. In his *Director*, Chippendale gives a few hints on decoration in the text accompanying the plates: 'They[chairs] are usually covered with the same Stuff as the Window-Curtains'. As a leading designer and cabinet-maker, Chippendale operated in three distinct ways: at his premises in St. Martin's Lane there was a range of ready-made furniture for customers to choose from; he acted as a decorator/designer and was able to advise clients and supply virtually everything that was necessary for the decoration of a room or a house [pl. 113]; and he executed commissions for top quality pieces designed by architects such as Robert Adam.

Very grand rooms were still hung with damask [pl. 106] and Robert Adam used Gobelins tapestry with specially designed furniture covered en suite in several luxurious rooms. The tapestries were bought by the clients and Adam successfully designed the rooms round them in the neo-classical taste [pl. 112]. Wallpaper manufacturers followed the fashion by introducing patterns of stripes and geometric forms, and paper – as a more usual and inexpensive method of decoration – was often supplied and hung by upholsterers [pl. 97]. There were various methods of doing this, one of the earliest being just to nail or tack the paper onto the plaster – a method that continued well on into the eighteenth century. Alternatively the paper could be pasted on, as it is today. The third method was to paste the paper onto scrim or canvas, batten out the room and then tack the backing and paper onto the battens; this technique was also used for textile hangings. The tacks or nails were hidden by braid or a fillet [pl. 89] – a fashion that started in the 1730s and that continued until the nineteenth century. The fillets were a definite part of the decorative scheme, following closely round the door architraves and fireplace mouldings, and merited the attention of designers such as Robert Adam and Thomas Chippendale, who actually gives ten designs for borders in the *Director*. The finest were in carved and gilded wood but they were also made of cast lead, papier mâché, composition or even cord dipped in gesso and then painted or gilded.

Print rooms became fashionable around the mid-eighteenth century. They were made by cutting out prints or engravings and pasting them onto plain coloured walls; blue, yellow, green

and even pink have been recorded as suitable background colours. These rooms provided a splendid opportunity to display the owner's excellent taste in the selection of the prints and in their arrangement. Sometimes they were planned by amateurs but the more elaborate examples were generally professionally designed – Chippendale was certainly responsible for at least one print room, alas now lost. Horace Walpole had such a room, which he describes in a letter of 1753 as 'a bed-chamber, hung with yellow paper and prints, framed in a new manner, invented by Lord Cardigan; that is, with black and white borders printed'. These ready-printed borders, and also swags, cords and bows, could be bought and arranged as desired to frame and 'hang' the prints [pl. 115]. In 1771, Mrs

115. The Print Room at Woodhall Park was designed in 1782 by one R. Parker whose drawings have been preserved. All the borders, ornaments, nails, festoons and pendants are on printed paper.

116. Hall at Heveningham by James Wyatt, 1780–4. The line of the barrel vault ribs is carried down the walls by pilasters and in bands across the elaborately patterned red and black marble and stone floor. The walls and ceiling are painted in shades of apple green and white, the pilasters and columns in yellow scagliola.

117. George Dance's experiment with pendentive vaulting together with the complex neo-classical plasterwork still retains its original decoration of about 1780.

Lybbe Powys visited Fawley Court in Buckinghamshire where she noted, 'On the left of the saloon is a large billiard-room hung with the most beautiful pink India paper, adorn'd with very good prints, the borders cut out and the ornaments put on with great taste by Bromwich, and the pink colour, besides being uncommon, has a fine effect under prints.' Print rooms continued to be constructed during the first decades of the nineteenth century – when the Duke of Wellington was given Stratfield Saye in 1817, he found print decoration in the gallery and became so enamoured of the idea that he adorned several other rooms in this fashion and signed each one with a print of himself.

It must be said that Robert Adam's great talent declined somewhat during the last fifteen years of his life. From the late 1770s his decorative work appears increasingly fussy, thin and mechanical in comparison with his early masterpieces. By 1780 he was losing commissions to James Wyatt [pl. 116] and Henry Holland, two of the most successful of the succeeding generation of neo-classical architects who, like William Chambers before them, used neo-classical ornament more fastidiously and sparingly than Adam. Adam's involvement in speculative schemes in Portland Place and the Adelphi in London ended in financial disaster and this, together with Wyatt's and Holland's success, drove him back for the last ten years of his life to his native Scotland, where he died in 1792.

Of the fourteen houses Adam designed in Scotland eight were in the 'castle' style, the 'picturesque' nature of which was itself an early portent of the gradual decline that was to afflict classical architecture fatally in the next century. James Wyatt also occasionally built in the 'castle' style but far more important than his 'castles' and even his neo-classical houses were those he designed in the Gothic style. His knowledge of authentic medieval buildings clearly distinguished his designs from the charming and frivolous essays of Rococo Gothic. Throughout the latter half of the 1700s Horace Walpole's taste for the Gothic was developing from its Rococo beginnings in 1748 to his final additions to Strawberry Hill in 1790, for which he employed the architect and antiquarian James Essex. Walpole, Essex and Wyatt, in their romantic quest for a medieval past, were in their way just as important precursors of the Romantic movement, if not more so, as Robert Adam and his fellow neo-classicists.

6

THE ROMANTIC VIEW

The Romantic movement in England broadly covers that period which in architecture, decoration and furniture we know as Regency (by 1785 the future Prince Regent had established his role as a royal arbiter of taste with his alterations to Carlton House). As we have seen, it had its roots in the archaeological approach that men like Robert Adam and James Stuart brought to their study of the classical remains of Europe and the Near East and Horace Walpole's similar approach to the medieval artefacts of his own country.

During the last decade of the eighteenth century the classical disciplines imposed by the Rule of Taste were breaking down. The Romantic movement brought about a revolution in the way people lived in their houses and the old, formal pattern of living gave way to informality. By 1826 a visitor to England

118. *Capt. Jessamy Learning the Proper Discipline of the Couch*, a satirical print of 1782, indicating the relaxation of formal manners. The curtains have the centre tassel usual at this time.

119. *Ensign Rosebud Reposing himself after the Fatigues of the Parade*, c.1782. The summer case cover on the couch is in a floral pattern, the flowers and vase in the grate could be real or a painted chimney board. The obelisk on the mantelshelf would be one of a pair.

INTERIORS

wrote, 'The practice of half lying instead of sitting; sometimes of lying at full length on the carpet at the feet of ladies; of crossing one leg over the other in such a manner as to hold the foot in the hand; of putting the hands in the arm-holes of the waistcoat, and so on, are all things that have obtained in the best company and the most exclusive circles.' This may be taking informality to an extreme but it underlines the enormous change that was taking place in 'polite' manners during this period [pls. 118, 119].

The visual ingredient of the Romantic movement was, essentially, the new fashion for the Picturesque, and at first this largely affected the external appearance of houses and the design of their surrounding gardens and parks. When Richard Payne Knight, the most formidable proponent of the Picturesque movement, designed a castle for himself at Downton in 1775 the exterior was unique at that time in being asymmetrical. Inside, however, the rooms were severely classical. By 1795, when the architect John Nash and the landscape gardener Humphrey Repton had committed themselves to Payne Knight's cause, the effects of the Picturesque were discernible inside the house. Inevitably, the Picturesque asymmetry of the castle and the equally fashionable 'ornamental' cottage would have to have suitable forms of decoration inside to reflect their exterior pretensions.

Repton, who was responsible for bringing the flower garden back into the immediate vicinity of the house, was to provide a new addition to houses in the form of the conservatory, which, by its very nature, furthered the essential asymmetry that fashion decreed. One such conservatory features prominently in the illustration of his 'modern living room' which he contrasts with 'the ancient cedar parlour' [pl. 120]. These two interior views and the accompanying verse provide perhaps the most lucid and succinct commentary on the changes in the use and arrangement of rooms that occurred around 1800.

The library, which throughout the eighteenth century had been a male preserve (and would revert to that in Victorian times), was used by the whole family [pl. 121]. In the 1790s, when Jane Austen was writing the first draught of *Pride and Prejudice*, Mr Bennet was 'discomposed exceedingly' by being followed into his library by the tiresome Mr Collins: 'In his

120. From Humphrey Repton's 'Fragments', 1816:
'No more the *Cedar Parlour's* formal gloom with dulness chills, 'tis now the *Living-Room*; where guests, to whim, or taste, or fancy true, Scatter'd in groups, their different plans pursue.'

121. The Great Library at Cassiobury being used as a living-room in the early nineteenth-century. Note the swagged curtains, the furniture arrangement and the fitted carpet in a geometric pattern with a wide border.

library he had always been sure of leisure and tranquillity; and though prepared, as he told Elizabeth, to meet with folly and conceit in every other room in the house, he was used to being free from them there.' In his *Collected Fragments*, which was published in 1816, Repton says that 'the most recent modern custom is, to use the library as the general living room; and that sort of state room, formerly called the best parlour, and, of late years, the drawing room, is now generally found a melancholy apartment, when entirely shut up, and only opened up to give visitors a formal cold reception: but, if such a room opens into an adjoining one, and the two are fitted up with the same carpet, curtains etc., they then become, in some degree, one room; and the comfort of that which has books, or musical instruments, is extended in its space to that which has only sofas, chairs and card tables; and then the living room is increased in dimensions, when required, with a power of keeping a certain portion detached, and not always used for common purposes.' The opening up of these two rooms would, Repton advised, be achieved with large folding doors (Nash was using large sliding doors at this time), but Repton also extended this to a suite of three or four rooms and this 'vista through a modern house' he says 'is occasionally increased by a conservatory at one end and repeated by a large mirror at the opposite end'. The fourth room Repton listed was the breakfast room, a comparatively new addition that had resulted from the importance this meal assumed towards

122. A design by Gillow & Co. dated 30 July 1819. The very elaborate 'continued' drapery of the curtains and the French-style cabinets between the windows suggest a rich client, while the furniture placed in the centre of the room indicates an advanced taste. (Victoria and Albert Museum, London.)

the end of the eighteenth century [pl. 129].

The change of use of rooms like the library and the addition of rooms like the breakfast room and conservatory was accompanied by loss of status in others; the saloon, the most lavishly decorated room in eighteenth-century houses, was downgraded to being what was termed 'an apartment of communication'. Such a dismissal of the great room of state in favour of the rooms that were used – the library, drawing-room and dining-room – provides a vivid example of the changes that were taking place. All the stress was now laid on convenience and comfort rather than on ceremony and this was inevitably extended to include the way in which the actual furniture was disposed in the rooms.

Sofas, formerly placed against walls, were now arranged at right angles to or facing the fireplace. The newly introduced sofa table was designed to stand in front of a sofa and to be used for reading or writing. The chairs, which formerly were replaced against the walls after use, now remained firmly in position. One contemporary correspondent unacquainted with this new fashion was convinced that her hostess's servants had left, when she saw the chairs scattered around the room. The new and important round or square pedestal table, often covered with a cloth, was frequently placed in the centre of the room [pls. 122, 123]. These were sometimes referred to as breakfast tables but large rectangular tables with tilt tops were also made specifically for the new breakfast parlours.

123. Drawing-room at Woolley Hall, with wall paintings of classical landscapes by Agostino Aglio, *c.*1818. The casual arrangement of furniture, the large double-doors connecting the suite of rooms, the plants in the window and the murals achieve precisely the effect that Repton and others were proposing.

This was a period when much new and specialist furniture was introduced, such as quartetto tables, canterburies to accommodate the plethora of magazines, ladies' work tables, chiffoniers and so on. Book storage was catered for in many novel ways, including the dwarf bookcase, which, according to George Smith, 'left ample space on the wall above for pictures' – these bookcases often had doors of wire mesh behind which was pleated silk of a suitable colour [pl. 124]. Libraries were fitted with continuous runs of shelving broken only at fireplaces and doors. Graining to imitate dark wood was often used by those who could not afford the preferred mahogany for their bookcases. *Chaises-longues* assumed a new importance and the Regency taste for producing a feeling of light and space was achieved by the lavish use of mirrors of all kinds, such as the newly introduced circular convex mirrors. 'By the aid of mirrors we multiply the costly embellishments that surround us, extend the apparent dimensions of our rooms and create the most magical effects,' wrote John Britton in 1827.

124. Mary Ellen Best painted her uncle in his study between 1837 and 1839. This comfortable room is furnished with a sofa and cushions in striped case covers and a chiffonier with brass mesh doors backed with fabric. The arrangement of the contemporary pictures in gilt frames is typical of the middle years of the nineteenth century

Satinwood, pale gold in colour, was much favoured by cabinet-makers until about 1800, when it was supplanted by rosewood and other showily marked woods. Painted furniture was often grained to imitate the fashionable but expensive woods such as maple, rosewood and zebra wood. Sometimes furniture was painted to complement decorative schemes and clients were asked to supply wallpaper and fabric patterns as samples. Painted or japanned seat furniture was generally caned – George Hepplewhite in 1788 says 'japanned chairs should have cane bottoms with linen or cotton cases over cushions to accord with the general hue of the chair'. Morocco leather, velvet or rich damask silk was recommended as covering for chairs and couches. More economically, Manchester (i.e. cotton) velvet or chintz might be used. As seat furniture was now permanently placed out in the room the backs were upholstered in the same expensive fabrics. Case (or loose) covers, which were in place nearly all the time, were chosen to harmonize with the general colour scheme – often two different sets were in use, one for summer and one for winter [pl. 124].

The taste for French furniture, which had first become fashionable in the 1760s with the introduction of neo-classicism, was given further impetus by George Prince of Wales when he began the remodelling of Carlton House. His architect, Henry Holland, had been in Paris before work on the house began in earnest in 1787. Holland's decoration, with its elegant interweaving of Greco-Roman and Louis XVI themes, formed a perfect background to the prince's growing collection of French furniture. The ornament here was controlled within panels or bands and used sparingly, in contrast with much of Robert Adam's work. Horace Walpole used the

125. This drawing by Jirouard Le Girouardy is dated 1789 and inscribed 'London, Decoration of the Room at Carlton House'. Le Girouardy was one of several French artists working under Henry Holland at Carlton House; he also worked at Inveraray Castle, Argyll.

126. French flock wallpaper 'Les deux pigeons', c.1785, by Reveillon, in whose factory a riot in 1789 sparked off the French Revolution. This paper is hung in the Palladio Room at Clandon Park.

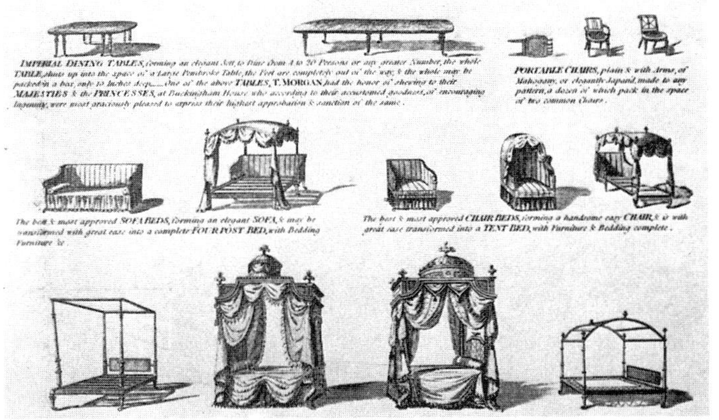

127. The trade card of an upholsterer and cabinet-maker operating 1803–17, showing some novel furniture such as portable, collapsible chairs and beds.

word 'chaste' in describing Holland's work – a term of genuine approbation [pl. 128].

If Holland's decoration was chaste, John Soane, who started his career in Holland's office, took the process of simplification almost to the point of abstraction. Soane's use of linear ornament was frequently accomplished by incisions in the surfaces of walls, ceilings and fireplaces. In his early, often modest, houses he created a whole range of decorative details – cornices, fireplaces, mouldings for doors – which were simple, yet refined and effective. They were to form a vocabulary of detail that was to be used in countless small Regency houses to create a reticent architectural framework for the rest of the decoration [pls. 129, 131].

The influence of French furniture and decoration on English taste was still considerable despite the Revolution and the outbreak of war in 1793. Indeed, between 1793 and 1815 any break in hostilities was eagerly seized upon to garner the new ideas that Paris had to offer. During the months that followed the Peace of Amiens in 1802 until the resumption of the war, the English flocked to Paris. Napoleon's brief incarceration on Elba in 1814-15 provided another opportunity – this time with the added bonus of a chance to see on display in the Louvre the emperor's spoils of war from all over Europe. From the first interlude the English would have brought back ideas culled from the *Directoire* style and from the second they would have had their first sight of the furniture and decoration of

128. The Boudoir, Southill designed by Henry Holland, *c.*1796. The panels (originally hung with green and white satin) are framed with gilt and ebonized mouldings. Note the bands of decoration on the ceiling and on either side of the mirror which was designed by Holland as was the pair of tiered bookcases.

the 'Empire' style. On either occasion they would have been able to buy copies of *Recueil des Decorations Interieures* which was published from 1801 in serial form and as a book in 1812. The authors of this work were Charles Percier and Pierre-Francois-Leonard Fontaine. In France their greatest surviving work is the Château de la Malmaison, which they decorated for Napoleon and Josephine.

The influence of Percier and Fontaine in England was considerable, not least in the promotion of their ideas through the pages of Ackerman's *Repository of Arts, Science etc.* [pl. 135]. This

magazine, which in its heyday had a readership of 2,000, was started in 1809 and ran until 1828. Among other articles it contained a 'Fashionable Furniture' feature which showed furniture and furnishings in all the various popular styles. It included work by such distinguished designers as George Bullock, Augustus Charles Pugin and his son Augustus Welby and also much from George Smith's *A Collection of Designs for Household Furniture and Decoration.* Not surprisingly, the work of Percier and Fontaine was not promoted until Napoleon was safely ensconced on St. Helena.

The handling of fabric and draperies reached new heights during the Regency period – perhaps inspired by the extraordinary tent rooms and draped walls designed by Percier and Fontaine. Their use of so much drapery to achieve astonishing decorative effects may have been the result of working under

pressure – the emperor was notoriously impatient. This fashion spread to England, so much so that a celebrated amateur was quoted as saying that 'he would be quite satisfied if a well proportioned barn was provided, and he would in a week convert it, by such means [ornamental finishing by draperies], into a drawing-room of the first style and fashion' [pls. 132, 133].

As a result of this great interest in drapery the design of curtains came to play a major role in decorative schemes at this time and until the late 1830s. From early in the century the aim of decorators and upholsterers had been to give a unity to the fenestration. To this end, the drapery was often carried across all the windows and was known as continued drapery [pl. 131]. The usual method of achieving this was to hang a

129. Sir John Soane's breakfast room of *c.*1796 would have been used as a library and study at later times of the day. Soane was George Dance's pupil and continued his experiments with vaulting – (see pl. 117).

130. An illustration from Ackerman's *Repository* shows a retail glass shop with a huge choice of lighting fittings as well as other goods such as tableware and vases.

131. This painting of the dining-room at Goldrood in 1848 shows rather old-fashioned decoration – the 'continued' curtain drapery was by now out of date. Note the windows down to floor level and the étagère of a plain, early-nineteenth-century shape. Note also the floorcloth, the small landscape mirror and the pair of bell pulls.

pole across the entire width and then drape material round it, either in graceful folds or very elaborate pointed drops. The drapes and curtains were often lined in a contrasting colour that was skilfully revealed by the draping. The curtains were nearly always floor length or cut to trail and were looped up during the day on cords or, more fashionably, on cloak pins [pl. 134]. French rods, which came in at the end of the eighteenth century, enabled the curtains to overlap when drawn. The frequent mention of curtain schemes as 'French' refers to the use of these rods rather than the actual design. Often there were inner curtains made of muslin and these, too,

were looped up on cloak pins. These inner curtains were often elaborately trimmed with fringe or embroidered borders or had scalloped edges. Edges cut in a V pattern, like Vandyke collars, were also much favoured for drapes and main curtains.

Almost every window was fitted with blinds made in various forms, from wooden slats that let in more or less light by altering the angle, to spring blinds of patterned chintz or painted cotton. In Gothic schemes the blind was sometimes painted to imitate the stained glass, heraldic or otherwise, of the window itself [pl. 136]. Sometimes the curtains were so elaborate that it was extremely difficult to draw them, in which case

132 (*opposite*). Although this tent room was formed in the very early 1830s it owes much to the inspiration of the work of Percier and Fontaine. It is wonderfully preserved and still hung with the original charming pink floral silk. Note the mirror glass above the light fitting as smoke protection as well as for reflection.

133 (*top left*). A detail of Plate 132 showing the attention that was lavished on the exquisite detail of this enchanting little room.

134 (*left*). The Blue Velvet Closet at Carlton House, which was remodelled in 1811. The harmony of the decoration – blue velvet panels, fitted carpet patterned with fleur-de-lis, and blue upholstery and curtains – provided a sumptuous background for the French furniture collected by the Prince Regent. (Guildhall Library, City of London.)

135 (*above*). Suggestions for drawing-room curtains from Ackerman's *Repository* for 1815. Note also the large window panes, thin glazing bars and the 'romantic' scenery.

the blinds would be used at night, but normally these were for use during the day to protect the expensive materials of the curtains and upholstery from fading.

In 1820, poles with elaborate drapes began to go out of fashion and were replaced by pelmets and pelmet boards. These accorded well with the growing fashion for Gothic

decoration and lent themselves to ornamentation with Gothic motifs such as crockets, ogee arches and so on [pl. 147]. A wide variety of materials was used for curtains, from extremely expensive velvet, silk and satin, sometimes figured but more often in plain colours, to Manchester velvet and calico – a term that embraced a large number of cotton fabrics including chintz. The new Jacquard looms were producing increasing quantities of small patterned wool damasks that were very popular, as was moreen – a sort of worsted cloth with a watered finish. Printed cotton chintz was used from the beginning of the century and with the improvement in techniques of dyeing more realistic colours were available for floral designs.

Ackerman's was just one of a number of periodicals that were published during the Regency period that set out to provide a guide to taste for the general public. They gave information

136. This rare survival of a painted blind is at Oxburgh Hall and dates from around 1850.

137. The 'Flaxman' room from Thomas Hope's book *Household Furniture and Decoration*, with the marble statue of Aurora visiting Cephalus. The colours of the decoration reflected the subject – black (night), orange (sunrise) and blue (sky).

on how to decorate and also what to buy and how to arrange it. These magazines were aimed at the amateur and the new rich. In an age of marked individualism it was, perhaps, not surprising that the amateur played an important part.

One of the most famous of these amateurs was the rich collector Thomas Hope, who was influenced by Percier's and Fontaine's book to the extent that he set out to emulate it by the publication of his own *Household Furniture and Decoration*, which appeared in 1807 [pl. 137]. Hope's exceptionally long Grand Tour of eight years had taken in Spain, Turkey, Syria, Greece and Egypt as well as France, Germany and Italy. Hope turned to Grecian ornament rather than the Roman favoured by Percier and Fontaine when he came to design the interior of his London house in Duchess Street. It is the decoration and furniture he designed for this house that is the subject of his book. Whilst Greece was the inspiration for most of the rooms there was also an Indian room and one inspired by Egypt. Hope also had an Egyptian room in his country house, the Deepdene.

From 1815 to 1821, John Nash had transformed the Royal Pavilion at Brighton into a Moghul fantasy for the Prince Regent. Here Indian details were frequently interwoven with the Chinese in decoration designed by Frederick Crace and Robert Jones in 1815 [pl. 138]. The influence of ideas from the past and, in particular, from the Near and Far East resulted in a huge and confusing choice of styles. However, as a result of this Romantic interest in the past, the English love affair with the Gothic was pursued with renewed vigour. With the addition of Norman at one end of the Gothic era and Elizabethan at the other, the spectrum of choice was wide

138. The corridor in the Brighton Pavilion in 1815. Note the pink drugget and the hearth rug.

enough to satisfy the most ardent romantic in his quest for a golden age. Nevertheless countless numbers of Regency terraced houses and villas built at this time had architectural details of decoration which displayed the unpretentious classicism derived from architects like Soane.

The Napoleonic wars, in accelerating the Industrial Revolution, made a rapidly expanding middle class richer. A large proportion of wealth was spent on new villas and houses with a resulting boom in speculative building, not only in London and the provincial towns, but in spa towns like Cheltenham and the newly fashionable seaside towns on the south coast. The use of cheap bricks with stucco lowered the cost of the structure and this was paralleled in the decoration by the production of cheaper wallpapers, fabrics and floor coverings. Other economies were effected by the paring down of architectural details such as cornices, architraves and fireplaces [pl. 140]. One important aspect of these light and simple interiors was the increase in the size of the windows (the window tax, introduced in 1696, was reduced for the first time in 1815). Ground-floor windows had been extended and lowered to just above the floor level in the 1760s and, with Repton's introduction of the flower-bedecked terrace, the French window was a natural and practical development. At the same time glazing bars were becoming thinner.

Apart from windows, other architectural features in Regency houses show a marked divergence from former prac-

139. A very complete Regency room in the 'Chinese' taste. The colour scheme is blue and gold with blue walls on which are framed hand-painted Chinese silk panels. These original curtains are gold damask edged with blue, the Chinese carpet is blue and gold and the table top is lapis lazuli.

140. A bedroom at Goldrood, *c.*1840. It is being used as a sitting-room by the ladies of the house. The bed valance and curtains match the window curtains, which are held back by cloak pins.

tice. Fireplaces are lower and tend to project further into the room following French models. Cornices, even in grand rooms, begin to trespass onto the ceilings. In general these features display an elegance in the smaller houses, in marked contrast to their more opulent counterparts where the heaviness and even crudeness of such details becomes increasingly apparent towards the end of the period, in both Greek revival and Gothic examples. It was in the smaller, less important rooms that the refined elegance reminiscent of the work of Holland and Soane was perpetuated.

Panels containing Chinese wallpaper, patterned silk or damask became fashionable and there are also cases of geometrically patterned papers being used in panels, the surrounds of which were sometimes grained [pl. 139]. Wallpapers of all kinds were used in profusion during the Regency period, partly from motives of economy and partly through improvement in the quality of papers available. Technical improvements such as cylinder printing machines and continuous sheet paper had lowered the price and increased production. Papers were so cheap that they were often changed every four or five years in lesser rooms [pl. 140]. The popular 'sprig' papers were supplemented by floral designs and small geometric patterns – sometimes with toning borders. Many of these papers were grounded on tiny all-over patterns that were advertised as an effective camouflage for fly spots. Moiré papers imitating watered silk were used for bedrooms where they were not hung with floral or chintz patterns. Halls and staircases were often hung with marble paper with a high gloss finish, giving a hard-wearing surface and the appearance of richness.

Rich flock papers were supplied for drawing-rooms, dining-rooms and libraries. These very good quality papers were made to last and were put up with great care, generally with elaborate fillets similar to those used for silk hangings. Alternatively, paper borders were used, such as the Greek key fret pattern in the gallery at Temple Newsam, put up in 1828 with the new red flock paper. The same pattern was sometimes used for flock and printed paper, with the flock destined for the grander rooms and the printed for lesser apartments. Authentic Chinese papers made a come-back with the renewed fashion for chinoiserie but English printed wallpapers were also designed to complement oriental decoration [pl. 142].

The addition of the conservatory was one of the most attractive new features of the period. These were nearly always placed to open out of the drawing-room or library and even quite small houses could now boast of this improvement. The

141. The Birdcage Room at Grovelands. The house was designed by John Nash in 1798. The room is decorated to look like a birdcage in a garden and set in a landscape.

wish to bring the outside inside, originated by Repton, inspired rooms painted like the inside of aviaries or decorated with panoramic views [pl. 141]. In his *Decorative Painter's and Glazier's Guide*, Nathaniel Whittock gives illustrations and directions for painted architectural settings, with suitable views in both the Chinese and the Gothic taste. Strangely enough, the magnificent scenic wallpapers created by Joseph Dufour in Paris from 1807 onwards and so popular in France and America made no impact in England during the Regency.

It was not beneath the dignity of ladies to indulge in wall-papering their rooms or to know the correct method of colouring their walls. Jane Austen's sister-in-law, Martha Lloyd, gives a recipe for 'A Wash for Rooms' in two versions, one using blue indigo and the other for a buff colour using Dutch pink. The blue was considered a deterrent to flies while buff was a popular colour throughout the period. This was a time when amateur accomplishments came into their own – penwork was a technique used to decorate not only charming boxes but also quite large pieces of furniture; hand-painted velvet was used for cushions and curtains were often bordered with painted or stencilled flowers or running patterns of geometric motifs.

The main rooms were the subject of more ambitious schemes. During the first quarter of the century it was still fashionable to match the curtains to the upholstery, with the walls and floor coverings in toning colours. With the exception of Gothic rooms the colours were generally light, such as lemon yellow or lilac, but nearly always in a combination of two colours for curtains, with the white muslin sub-curtains providing a fresh contrast. The 'well approved harmony of colour constituted by blue, buff and white' is frequently mentioned while other popular combinations included blue and lilac, amber and French grey, and light green and pink. Cords, elaborate fringes and tassels were generally gold or yellow to pick up the gilding of the furniture and picture frames.

Colours were chosen with due consideration to the aspect of the rooms. Blue and green tones were considered suitable for south-facing chambers while those with a northerly aspect

142 (*opposite*). The Chinese Drawing-Room at Temple Newsam was decorated in 1827–8. It is hung with Chinese wallpaper given by the Prince Regent in 1806 which is embellished with birds cut out from spare bits of the paper and Audubon's *Birds of America*. The room was restored in 1987 and the carpet rewoven from a design of *c.*1824.

143 (*above*). 'Palm Tree and Pheasant' – a block-printed cotton in madder colours, *c.*1815, by Charles Swainson at Bannister Hall, a leading printer of furnishing textiles at this time.

144. The frieze and the border round the doorway in this room at A la Ronde are entirely made of feathers. These were executed by the Misses Parminter, builders of this unique early-nineteenth-century house. It is extensively decorated by them with shells, seaweed, sand, feathers and other unusual materials.

145. A rare survival from the early nineteenth century is this small room at Pencarrow hung with printed linen, with curtains and a box cornice to match.

were warmed with buff, pink or red tones – this was particularly true of bedrooms, where floral papers were preferred for north-facing rooms. Paintwork was generally coloured to match the ground of the paper. There were rules to be followed as George Smith points out, 'For Eating Rooms and Libraries, a material of more substance is requisite than for rooms of a lighter cast . . . the colours as fancy and taste may direct; yet scarlet and crimson will ever hold preference'. Red in all tones was the colour in general use for dining-rooms and libraries

and this would be carried through the curtains, upholstery and walls – a Turkey-pattern carpet or drugget on the floor would complete the scheme, for instance, 'Crimson drugget . . . panelled with a border of black furniture cloth, producing a warm, rich appearance'. However, there were plenty of original schemes of decoration, as in Lord Hertford's house described by a visitor in 1827: 'The singularity in it is, that all the rooms are decorated in the same manner – flesh coloured stucco and gold, with black bronze, very large looking-glasses, and curtains of crimson and white silk. This uniformity produces a very "grandiose" effect. One room alone (of extraordinary size for London) is white and gold, carpeted with scarlet cloth, and with furniture and curtains the same colour.'

Floor coverings were considered an integral part of the decoration and, as such, their designs followed or complemented prevailing fashions. These were most especially reflected in the Brussels and Wilton close carpeting that had been in fashion since the 1770s. Geometric patterns loosely based on Roman pavements were popular and designs were sometimes 'dropped' to give a more lively effect. In the 1820s Gothic designs featuring quatrefoils, tracery, cusping and so on became popular to complement the emerging fashion for Gothic decoration. Oriental rugs were out of fashion and did not become really popular again until the 1880s but 'Turkish' patterns were used for English carpets designed for libraries and dining-rooms. Hand-made rugs came into vogue again but now using geometrical patterns, although these were sometimes overlaid with sprays of flowers.

Specially designed bespoke carpets continued to be made for the luxury market and, as in the eighteenth century, these carpets would have had their own covers. However, more modest carpets also had covers; for instance, a client writing to Chippendale and Haig in 1789 specifies, 'You may remember you showed me some pieces of carpeting when I was in London and I made a choice of one. It was a large pattern and there was a good deal of yellow in it. There must be a covering for it of green serge.' Covers were also of baize and were frequently chosen to match the case covers of the furniture; cotton and linen drugget was often used in strips to cover the carpet where wear was most likely. Drugget and baize, sometimes with needlework borders, were also used on their own as a very cheap form of floor covering. Other cheap carpets were also available, in particular the reversible woven ingrain carpets made in Kidderminster and Scotland.

Oriental matting was used with chinoiserie decoration and became quite popular. By 1800 specialist dealers in carpets were appearing and shortly afterwards some manufacturers opened their own showrooms. The choice of stock patterns was left to the client – perhaps with advice from his architect or upholsterer.

With the first great schemes for Gothic decoration by James Wyatt at the end of the eighteenth century and such designs as William Porden's Eaton Hall the new re-creation of the Gothic style really got under way [pl. 147]. As the nineteenth century progressed this style became increasingly popular with the newly rich and completely eclipsed the more restrained fashion for the Greek revival. Rich, glowing colours such as crimson and sapphire blue with plenty of gold, reminiscent of

146. The faded fabric (seen in Plate 145), printed with exotic birds and bamboo, gives a hint of the original impact of this decoration.

illuminated manuscripts, were used for draperies and upholstery, and furniture and carpets were designed to make full use of the vocabulary of Gothic ornament. Armour was a favourite collector's item and extremely elaborate schemes were devised for showing it to best advantage. Stained and painted glass was used in windows and lanterns to give an effect of richness; and the use of heraldic glass 'proved' the ancient lineage of the owner – often one of the motives for choosing Gothic in the first place. Apart from the romantic appeal of the Gothic style it also came to have an association with 'godliness' and 'Englishness', which perhaps accounts for the overwhelming popularity of this form of decoration in the middle years of the nineteenth century.

147. The drawing-room, Eaton Hall, built by William Porden in 1802–26 in the full enthusiasm of the early-nineteenth-century taste for the Gothic. The colour scheme of intense crimson and blue is echoed in the stained-glass windows; the curtain treatment is particularly interesting.

7

THE BATTLE OF THE STYLES

Although early skirmishes in the 'Battle of the Styles', as it came to be called, had taken place in the first decades of the nineteenth century, by the 1830s all the signs of the ensuing chaos were already apparent. If the 'Greek' and 'Gothic' protagonists had abided by a strict interpretation of those styles the resultant anarchy might have been contained but through either a wilful disregard of historical accuracy or ignorance they enlisted every style that they could muster to serve their purpose. The 'Goths' used Norman, Elizabethan and Jacobean, none of which was Gothic, as indiscriminately as they used every aspect of the Gothic style itself – any style, in fact, which could remotely be considered representative of Old England. Meanwhile, under the Greek banner virtually every phase of classical architecture and decoration was deployed. In their interpretation of eighteenth-century French decoration, the 'Greeks' were unable or unwilling to distinguish between Louis XIV, Louis XV and Louis XVI, all of which styles were combined without distinction – a mesalliance that has been neatly described as Louis the Hotel.

Only a genius could hope to make sense out of the monstrous variety of styles available, and it is perhaps understandable that very few designers were single-minded, knowledgeable and gifted enough to rise above the increasingly dismal standard of Victorian decoration. Architects and designers are always at the mercy of their patrons but in this particular period they were working for a new type of client in an uncomfortably changing society. The aristocratic, visually educated patron of the eighteenth century was being replaced by clients whose wealth was seldom matched by their knowledge or taste. Between 1800 and 1850 the population in Britain doubled and the increase in the wealth of the country was even more dramatic. It might have been easier to assimilate the effect of these traumatic changes on the visual arts if the Rule of Taste had still applied. The Romantic movement, propounding self-expression and originality, had destroyed any hope of establishing such a cohesive set of rules. More importantly, it changed the way people looked at and judged their surroundings. The rational approach of the eighteenth century was supplanted by an emotional and literary one.

Jane Austen had satirized the Romantic movement in the last years of the eighteenth century; by the time *Northanger Abbey* was published in 1818, it is doubtful whether many people were able to look at a garden or a house dispassionately enough to divorce it from its literary associations. Jane Austen's great champion, Sir Walter Scott, alas, did not share the clarity of her vision. In transforming what had, in the 1750s, been a straightforward interest in the archaeological discoveries of the time into an all-consuming antiquarian involvement, Scott more than anyone else influenced and ultimately impaired the sight of both those who were to commission houses and those who were to design them. If we can enjoy and admire the interiors of his own Abbotsford, most later imitations warrant no such interest. The distorting gauze that Romanticism pulled over the eyes was reflected in such minor ways as the vogue of covering paintings in varnish – 'The Romantic amateur loves the rust and haze of the varnish for it has become a veil behind which he can see whatever he desires.' (Horsin Déon '*De la conservation*, 1851).

The lure of the past is, as we have seen, a constantly recurring theme but in the first half of the nineteenth century it had reached a level of such absurd proportions that it could be considered a disease – one from which we continue to suffer. In 1845 Ruskin complained that having escaped to the past 'some gas pipe business forces itself upon the eye, and you are thrust into the nineteenth century'. While succumbing to the malady, men such as the Gothic revival architect George Gilbert Scott were evidently fully aware of the danger: 'The effect of working with this vivid panorama of the past placed constantly in our view, is to induce a capricious eclecticism – building now in this style, now in that – content to pluck the flowers of history without cultivating any of our own.' Inspired by a patriotism fostered by Wellington's victories, and fuelled by a rapidly acquired snobbery that demanded instant ancestors, the new patrons turned to an older England which the antiquarians like Horace Walpole and Sir Walter Scott had discovered for them. As Sir John Summerson has pointed out, 'A love of antiquarianism is much easier to acquire than an eye for classical proportion.'

In their search for examples to copy and given a predisposition for elaborate decorative detail the antiquarians frequently had to turn to ecclesiastical buildings. Only in cathedrals and parish churches could they find the right precedents to satisfy them. The Romanesque detail at Penrhyn [pl. 152] was not to be found in a Norman castle, even if the inspiration to build it *was* found in the Norman castles of Sir Walter Scott's romance *Ivanhoe*. The Norman style, however, appealed to few, probably for the very good reason that it provided a comparatively limited vocabulary of decorative details.

There was far more scope in other areas of 'Olde England'. Over three hundred years of Gothic building yielded many more models with which to satisfy the most eclectic of tastes. Moreover, in its last phase it could include that important element, Tudor, within its orbit. The Tudor style had much to recommend it. Grand Tudor houses still existed, many with their decoration intact, whereas their medieval counterparts were extremely scarce. From the late Gothic of Henry VII's time to Elizabethan and Jacobean adaptations of Renaissance ornament [pl. 151], the sheer range of available decoration gathered together arbitrarily under the heading of Tudor gave the early nineteenth-century patrons and architects enormous scope to realize their dreams. This, together with the fact that many Elizabethan and Jacobean houses were, like later classical houses, symmetrically planned, may have contributed to the early revival of the style at a time when classicism was still a potent force, since the odd 'dull' Georgian house could have an exciting face-lift without having to be rebuilt.

The old Tudor houses were not only plundered for ideas – their fabric was far from safe [pl. 153]. Windows, doors, panelling and carving, stained glass and armour were eagerly sought out and bought. Horace Walpole was already in the market in the 1760s for stained glass or indeed anything else that he

148. Drawing-room (formerly the dining-room) at Eastnor Castle designed by Augustus Welby Pugin, *c.*1850. The painted decoration was carried out by the famous firm of Crace, who also made the table and chairs at the far end of the room to Pugin's design. He copied the chandelier from one in Nuremberg Cathedral.

thought was historically or romantically interesting enough for Strawberry Hill. By the 1820s a flourishing trade existed to cater for the growing demand for all such decorative items, as well as furniture. The dealers or nicknackitarians and brokers, as they were called, set up their 'old curiosity shops' in London, concentrating on Soho and the adjacent area north of Oxford Street. Every facet of the antique trade that we know today existed then, including those less desirable aspects such as widespread faking and the pernicious dealer rings at auctions. Sotheby's, Christie's and Phillips were the foremost auctioneers but there were a number of others as well to handle the flood of goods, much of which came from the Continent. France after the Revolution proved a particularly fruitful source of supply of medieval artefacts to the richest nation in the world. Carved woodwork, armour and stained glass from Europe ended up in Tudor and Gothic revival houses. The architect Augustus Welby Pugin even had his own ship for Continental forays to supplement his purchases at home, which he either sold to dealers or incorporated in houses like Scarisbrick, where the display of armour forms an important part of the decoration of the great hall [pl. 149].

149 (*above*). Design for the 'medieval' Great Hall at Scarisbrick by Augustus Welby Pugin, *c.*1840. Armour, probably to be supplied by Pugin himself, is displayed on the fireplace and a great buffet stands between the two doors of the screen.

150 (*top right*). The King's Room at Scarisbrick was one of the most richly decorated in the house. Portraits of kings and queens are incorporated in the panelling.

151. Richard Bridgens's design, of 1838, for a 'Tudor' window treatment.

152 (*opposite*). Thomas Hopper copied details from Castle Hedingham (see pl. 7) when he designed the Norman castle at Penrhyn in 1827. Elliptical instead of round arches (on the left-hand wall) indicate that he had not mastered Romanesque architecture. He also introduced 'Norman' skylights. The stained glass was designed by Thomas Willement.

As a visual expression of romantic chivalry, armour was considered an essential element in the great hall, which in itself was a symbol of medieval hospitality and revelry. Very elaborate schemes were worked out for the display – in his new medieval castle at Goodrich Sir Samuel Rush Meyrick even built an armoury in 1828 to house his famous collection. If armour was not available in sufficient quantity it was simulated in papier mache or ceramic; however, neither Sir Samuel nor Pugin would ever have countenanced such deceit.

Pugin's grasp of Gothic detail was much greater than his predecessors' or his contemporaries' [pl. 150], and unlike them he was passionately convinced of the superiority of the Gothic. All other styles he considered to be pagan. In championing Gothic as English but, above all else, Christian he brought God into the Battle of the Styles on the side of the 'Goths', contributing to their eventual victory over the 'Greeks'. People who were just becoming accustomed to looking at buildings through a Romantic haze were, by the beginning of Victoria's reign in 1837, expected to judge architecture in terms of its moral virtues. As always, these new conceptions were at first confined to large houses, only percolating down the scale, in an increasingly vitiated form, towards the middle of the century.

In contrast to the pomposity of many of these houses, the interiors of smaller houses and villas in the towns, the new suburbs and the country were refreshingly unpretentious [pl. 154], their owners uninterested in the ancestor worship of their wealthier compatriots. Although the details of architectural decoration became steadily more ponderous than those of the Regency period they remained sensibly simple and practical. The opening in a fireplace was often near semi-circular in shape rather than rectangular. The overall proportion of the fireplace, however, remained low and was usually sur-

153. The hall at Gawthorpe was largely redecorated by Sir Charles Barry, *c.*1850. He repaired and extended the screen to include the incongruous corner sections to display blue and white ceramics. The 1605 ceiling was reconstructed to include Barry's 'improvements'. The curtain fabric was designed by A.W. Pugin.

mounted by a very large mirror, adding to that particular quality of lightness that is characteristic of classical Regency and early Victorian interiors [pl. 160]. This quality was further enhanced by the increased size of windows and the introduction of plate glass, which although first produced in England in 1773 only became commercially viable when a method of polishing it was invented in 1838. It is a telling comment on the folly of the time that the possibilities of plate glass were neglected or misunderstood. The owners of the by now despised eighteenth-century houses were ripping out the carefully proportioned glazing bars and substituting huge single sheets of plate glass; while the designers of the new 'medieval' houses ignored the potential of plate glass altogether and were, perforce, reducing the window openings with Tudor mullions and transoms or Gothic shafts and filling them with stained glass.

The greatest specialist in stained glass was Thomas Willement, whose working career stretched from 1812 to 1865. He was appointed 'heraldic artist' to George IV and later 'artist in stained glass' to Queen Victoria. In 1840 he published *A Concise Account of the Principal Works in Stained Glass*. The Regency interest in stained glass and heraldry had been aroused partly by the wish of the newly rich to establish a 'background' for their families and partly by the rise of the Gothic style. The Tudor revival sparked interest in a number of hitherto neglec-

154. The classical architectural details of this room – fireplace, cornice and architrave to the large opening – lack the refinement of Sir John Soane's earlier models but are relatively simple and unpretentious. Note the colsa oil chandelier and the landscape mirror over the fireplace.

IVE TO LEARN LEARN TO LIVE

ted Elizabethan and Jacobean houses, many of which contained stained glass, and Willement was frequently consulted about the restoration of the glass. It was for this that he was first summoned to Charlecote, but he was soon consulted about the redecoration of the house and he worked there for about ten years from 1829 [pls. 155, 156]. Willement acted as a traditional upholsterer, supplying wallpapers, many of which he designed, carpets and curtains as well as antique and modern furniture. With his background knowledge of the medieval, he was just the man to appeal to the new antiquarian taste. The search for authenticity led to some curious results both in restoration [pl. 153] and in the purchase of 'antiques' – it was Horace Walpole who first bought Indo-Portuguese chairs under the delusion that they were Elizabethan, a myth that was perpetuated in a number of nineteenth-century country houses.

Although the eighteenth-century Rule of Taste was overthrown in the nineteenth century, other rules relating to other aspects of decoration and based on scientific theories were considered just as important. Some of these ideas had far-reaching results – in particular, those relating to colour. Isaac Newton had split the spectrum into seven hues and towards the end of the eighteenth century these colours, minus indigo, were published as red opposite green, purple opposite yellow and orange opposite blue. In 1810 Goethe became interested and reordered the spectrum, concluding that blue was next to darkness and yellow next to light. Many theories followed and were applied to decorating. For instance, blue made a room look cold and larger; green was completely neutral and therefore a common choice for everyday rooms.

In 1844 David Hay published his book *Laws of Harmonious Colouring Adapted to House Painting*, which introduced new ideas and codified them. Hay had started his career painting at Abbotsford for Sir Walter Scott but he soon became established as the leading decorator in Edinburgh. Some of the more unlikely colour combinations seen in the nineteenth century, for example yellow and purple with orange and yellowish green, owe their origin to Hay's theories. Later, he elaborated his theories to include the need to balance tone and brightness as well as colour. These ideas led to the abandonment of the universal white used for architectural mouldings in the eighteenth century.

In his book, David Hay also gave advice on decoration and rules on how to set about deciding on colour and style. Firstly, the tone was to be determined by the choice of furniture; then the warmth or coldness of colour would depend on the aspect and light of the apartment. The style of colouring was dependent on the use of the room – a drawing-room should have vivacity, gaiety and light cheerfulness, which would be introduced by tints of brilliant colours and a good degree of contrast and gilding, with the brightest colours and strongest tints in the furniture. With the invention of springing in the second

155. Thomas Willement decorated the library at Charlecote in 1833, designing the ceiling, bookcases, wallpaper and the fabric for the case covers as well as the carpet. The antique vases were purchased by the owner in 1829 and 1841.

156. Thomas Willement's wallpaper patterns preserved at Charlecote. Of the flock and metallic papers he warned his client 'the hanging of flock and metallic papers requires very great care'.

quarter of the nineteenth century and the lavish use of deep buttoning, seat furniture assumed a new dominance in decorative schemes. The Rococo revival had a strong effect on furniture design which persisted for many years – the ubiquitous balloon-back chair and extravagantly curved sofas and easy chairs date from this time. Upholstery and its colour and pattern became the most outstanding feature of drawing-rooms and parlours. Hay went on to make suggestions about the other rooms in the house, ending with staircases, lobbies and vestibules, which, he said, should be cool in tone to give an effect of architectural grandeur. The Regency fashion for imitation marble papers in these areas continued although paintwork in imitation of marble was now equally popular.

The firm of D.R. Hay developed a wide repertoire of painted finishes such as the 'patent imitation of damask'. He was especially successful in decoration in the 'Pompeian' style, which was recommended for lobbies and entrance halls. The interest in this type of wall painting dated from the new excavations at Pompeii in the late 1740s, and continued well on into the nineteenth century [pl. 157] – the 'Pompeian' room at Ickworth was not completed until 1879.

Another influential publication was John Claudius Loudon's *Encyclopedia of Cottage, Farm and Villa Architecture*. In this book, Loudon set forth his thoughts on architecture, of which the 'Italianate' was his preferred style. He gave even more detailed advice on decorating than David Hay – rose pink and green, for instance, was a highly recommended colour combination. He also went into practical detail on subjects such as the different colours and types of carpets for different rooms and how they should be laid 'showing about a yard all round it of the polished oak boards'. Floors were no longer dry scrubbed; highly polished oak floors, often stained a dark colour, date from the first half of the century.

From the time of its publication in 1836 until at least the 1860s Loudon's book wielded an important influence. One of his commands was that 'All woodwork [in cottages] should be grained in imitation of some natural wood.' The Regency had seen the return of marbling and the graining of furniture to imitate expensive woods. However, in the nineteenth century this kind of *faux* painting reached incredible heights of realism [pl. 158]. One of the greatest exponents was Thomas Kershaw, who won a first-prize medal at the Great Exhibition in 1851 for his 'Imitation of foreign and English marbles and wood, for house decorations; made of wood and slate'. At the International Exhibition of 1862 he showed painted imitations of embossed leather and silk damasks, one of which, in the Louis XVI style of rose silk, even deceived the distinguished decorator J.G. Crace [pl. 159]. During most of the nineteenth century graining of interior woodwork was normal practice and sets of graining combs and rollers were standard equipment.

157. Mid-Victorian version of 'Etruscan/Pompeian' painted decoration in a Somerset vicarage. Over the succeeding decades members of the family painted vignettes with which they embellished this decoration.

158. Design for wall decoration in the dining-room at Biddulph Grange, by John Gregory Crace, 1873, showing marbelized pilasters framing panels of 'Pompeian' decoration.

159. Detail of early Victorian marbelizing at Pencarrow House. Both local Cornish granite and Italian marble have been meticulously simulated. Late-seventeenth- and eighteenth-century marbelizing was deliberately less faithful to the original.

The Regency fashion of 'continued' drapery for window curtains lost ground after about 1820 and was replaced by pelmets or pelmet boards, or as in the early seventeenth century, the curtains were hung very simply from poles but using large, ornamental, wooden or metal rings. Box pelmets, sometimes of mahogany or sometimes painted, also appeared at this time. By the late 1830s stiffened pelmets had developed into arched lambrequins that displayed the heavy, shaded patterns produced by the early Victorian Jacquard weavers – these lambrequins were generally trimmed with a long fringe and the shape remained popular for most of the century [pl. 160].

The swags and drapes of Regency curtains were considered to be unhealthy, as they harboured dust and were difficult to clean. As a result, a strong vertical emphasis appeared in the pleats used not only for window curtains but also for the curtaining of beds. In about 1840 an unknown writer states categorically, 'Window curtains should always accord with the hanging on the bed, both in colour and material, and also in shape.' The elaborate mixtures of colours and materials that were used to give a strong decorative effect to window curtains in the early years of the nineteenth century were abandoned in favour of simpler draw curtains in one material – very often a Jacquard weave or, at the least, a fairly weighty material that would hang well and be suitable for pleated pelmets. Chintzes and printed cottons tended to be used in bedrooms and for bed curtains [pl. 161]. Trimming of fringing or *passementerie* was often replaced by contrasting edging made by folding the plain coloured lining forward over a printed fabric – a particularly successful decorative edging that has never gone out of fashion.

160. London drawing-room, 1836. The woman is writing at a sofa table behind which can be seen the fashionably new Rococo revival panelling. Note the large mirror over the fireplace and the large windows extending to the floor, with a few thin glazing bars framing large sheets of glass.

Many new designs for beds were developed at this time, including the half tester and beds with metal frames. Whatever the shape, however, they were invariably still hung with curtains – either white dimity or, more frequently, flowered chintz or cotton. These curtains would also often have stiffened pelmets cut to emphasize the pattern of the material or else vaguely 'Gothic' or 'Elizabethan' in shape, depending on the designated character of the room [pl. 165].

From about 1790, improvements in printing and dyeing techniques led to a vastly increased production of printed cotton goods – particularly in the early years as patterns were only protected by copyright for a few months. After 1842 when the British Copyright Act extended protection to three years, the quest for ever more new designs became less frenetic. The idea of offering patterns in several different colourways had first appeared around 1820 and from then on became quite usual. Technical improvements in printing continued and resulted in an explosion of brilliantly coloured, all-over-printed cottons of every variety. With the removal of taxation on prints in 1831, one- and two-colour unglazed cottons became very cheap and were used in quantity.

One of the more influential discoveries was that of quercitron – a fast yellow that, when overprinted with indigo, produced green. When the fifteen-year patent on the use of this dye expired in about 1800 'drab' colours became fashionable. The effect of printing green in this way was that the yellow tended eventually to fade, leaving the blue green that is characteristic of old patterns of this time [pl. 162]. During the 1840s there was a revival of interest in mid- and late-eighteenth-century designs and, although a fast solid green was by this time avail-

161. The same floral chintz has been used for curtains, bed and upholstered chairs in this mid-nineteenth-century bedroom and all three mirrors have Rococo frames. The small pattern of the wallpaper and the elaborate covering of the dressing-table add to the essential femininity of the room. (Watercolour by Samuel Rayner, Victoria and Albert Museum, London.)

162. A cotton print of pelargoniums from a bedroom at Pencarrow. This chintz dating from the 1840s deliberately imitates the fading of green to blue of earlier prints before a fast green dye had been discovered.

163. Three glazed printed cottons from the second quarter of the nineteenth century. The traditional design of ribbon with flowers is seen here in a rather debased form. From the textile collection at Temple Newsam.

164. Flowered wallpaper of the 1840s on a moiré background, from Pencarrow. The difference in colour is due to exposure – the lighter section shows the original appearance.

165. This bedroom at Pencarrow was decorated in the second quarter of the nineteenth century. The bed, chaise longue and armchair are all covered with chintz printed with roses and dahlias and only 24 inches (60 cm) wide.

able, it was considered more authentic to simulate the faded blue green that had resulted from the use of quercitron!

For about ten years from the 1820s, designers of floral prints for cottons created extremely realistic, beautifully drawn designs based on botanical publications but using completely unnatural colours. However, from the 1830s colours reverted to the naturalistic. Floral designs continued to be enormously popular – interest in the flower garden had been fostered by Repton, and the conservatories attached to so many Regency and Victorian houses had encouraged this interest. The large numbers of new flowers introduced to Britain at this time were frequently featured in textile designs. There was also a fashion for bird prints, many of them based on Audubon's *Birds of America*, which was published in London in 1827 and 1838. Game birds had been used as subjects in about 1810 [pl. 143] reflecting the increasing popularity of shooting. Pillar prints, stripes in every possible variety, prints imitating Berlin woolwork, prints designed to be cut and used as borders, as well as rosebud patterns of every kind proliferated during the second quarter of the nineteenth century [pl. 163].

The extraordinary variety of revivalist styles in architecture at this time was naturally echoed by the textile printers and weavers – for instance, the Rococo revival of the 1830s and 1840s (sometimes misleadingly called the Louis XIV style) that stimulated interest in English eighteenth-century patterns as well as French designs. In 1840 the decorators H.W. and A. Arrowsmith recommended the Tudor style as being 'well suited for a dining-room, the arabesque for sitting rooms, and the gorgeous French styles for drawing-rooms' [pl. 167]! Paning was revived but instead of evoking the seventeenth century it

166. A cotton 'pillar print' of the type that was extremely popular between 1825 and 1835. This one dates from the 1830s and is quite large scale – the reserves with portraits measure 6½ inches (16.5 cm) across. From the textile collection at Temple Newsam.

was looked on, quite wrongly, as being essentially medieval and Renaissance. The effect was achieved by stitching vertical bands of embroidery onto plain fabric to be used for curtains and seat upholstery. 'Mock' paning was also produced in woven fabrics.

Books and engravings had always been the most fertile source of inspiration for textile and wallpaper designers – Robert Adam's *Works in Architecture*, for instance, being one of the most widely plundered during the late eighteenth century. Many books of designs for ornament were published during the nineteenth century. Two of the most extensively copied were by Owen Jones – *Plans, Elevations, Sections and Details of the Alhambra* (1836-45) and his *Grammar of Ornament* (1856), which introduced stylized Moorish patterns and which had been reprinted nine times by 1910.

Wallpaper manufacture had also been enormously improved – by the first decade of the nineteenth century it was already possible to produce paper as wide as 54 inches (1.36m) and by mid-century steam-driven wallpaper printing machines were in general use. Devices for embossing and gilding were patented during the 1840s and 1850s. In 1836, the duty on paper staining was abolished and the duty on paper itself was reduced – all of which helped Britain to be at the forefront in the production of cheap papers.

During the 1840s floral sprigs, trellis and patterns based on textile designs were popular, many of them on a moiré ground that was considered especially suitable for bedrooms [pl. 164]. Papers in imitation of panelling and borders printed to simulate architectural mouldings such as 'egg and dart' were designed to appeal to the followers of the 'classical' style, where

167. London drawing-room, *c.*1855, showing the smart mid-century taste for the three Louis – reproduction Louis XIV Boulle cabinets, Louis XVI tables, and the Victorians' idea of Louis XV Rococo panelling in plaster. The Rococo plaster cornice begins at this time to seep onto the ceiling. (Watercolour by Samuel Rayner, Victoria and Albert Museum, London.)

wall spaces were often treated as if each were a huge panel, framed with paper borders or, in the advanced Rococo revival, with plasterwork. At the same time a large number of Gothic designs and geometric patterns were being produced to complement the Gothic style [pl. 168]. Wallpaper, like textiles designs, was also available in different colourways.

While manufacturers of textiles and wallpapers were producing vast quantities of new designs, architects like Augustus Welby Pugin were designing fabrics and papers for use by their own clients. Pugin's designs were frequently carried out by the firm of Crace with whom he had close associations – indeed, it was this firm that executed his designs for the Medieval Court at the Great Exhibition of 1851. The firm, spanning three generations of the same family, had started working for the Prince Regent in 1788 and had been responsible for much of the interior decoration of the Brighton Pavilion. It became one of the most important firms of interior decorators in the nineteenth century, supplying furniture, textiles and wallpapers and executing the work as well as advising clients in its own right.

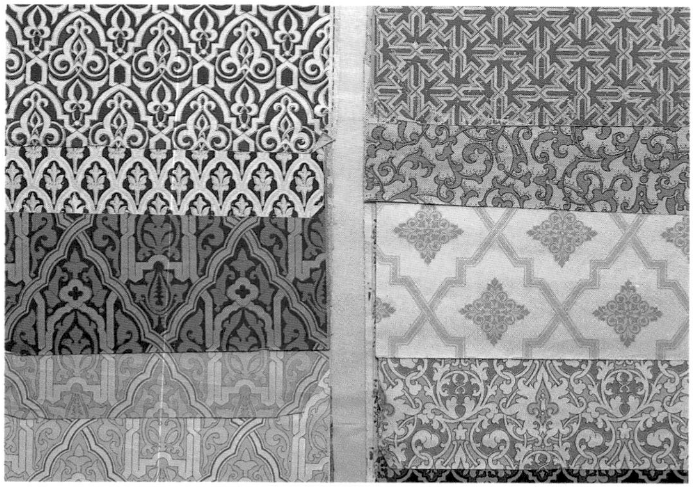

With the change to mass production of every item that could be required for the decoration and furnishing of a house the pattern of purchasing changed also. Except at the very top level, customers no longer ordered directly from the maker or producer; nor was it practical or desirable for them to visit the factory where the goods were made. A number of wallpaper manufacturers had already set up their own retail outlets, as had firms like Wedgwood and Gillows of Lancaster, both of whom were well established by the end of the eighteenth century. However, these individual enterprises were overtaken by the new stores that stocked a whole range of goods, and by the mid-nineteenth century names such as Maples, Shoolbred and Heal were well known in London. It was now possible for the customer to buy a vast range of ready-made goods and to assemble them in any way thought fit – an opportunity that certainly contributed to the muddled interiors of the period.

The technical mastery of mass production had opened up limitless scope for ornamentation and embellishment at relatively little extra cost. The unfortunate results were to be seen at the Great Exhibition. This brain-child of the Prince Consort, housed in the enormous Crystal Palace designed by Joseph Paxton and set up in Hyde Park, had been envisaged as an international exhibition of all that was best in modern manufactured goods. In the event, the Medieval Court designed by Pugin proved to be the most popular feature among the myriad exhibits. It was ironic that this exhibition only confirmed an already existing impression of the low standard of design in Britain; as early as 1835 a select committee under the chairmanship of the MP for Liverpool had been set up to 'inquire into the best means of extending a knowledge of the arts and of the principles of design among the people (especially the manufacturing population) of the country'. The exhibition also reinforced the horror of mechanical and mass production felt by certain artists, philosophers and designers that would lead in time to the foundation of the Arts and Crafts movement – a movement diametrically opposed to the principles of the Great Exhibition.

168. A series of wallpaper patterns of the second quarter of the nineteenth century, all from Ashburnham House where some but not all were used. From the collection at Temple Newsam.

8

CONFUSION AND NOSTALGIA

By the time of the Great Exhibition, the whole trend of design in interior decoration could only be described as hopelessly muddled. As we have seen in the early years of the nineteenth century, different styles of decoration were already in fashion simultaneously – a trend that gathered momentum throughout the century so that there was never a clear pointer in any one direction [pl. 169]. The choice of goods was so wide, the conflicting styles so many, and the advice from the numerous books and articles on the subject so great, that the average person who wished to decorate a house or even one room must have been completely confused [pl. 171].

Owen Jones was responsible for the paintwork of the Crystal Palace at the Great Exhibition. He subsequently wrote *Principles of Employment of Colour*, which puts forward a number of propositions and seems to sum up what had been happening in architectural education: 'As each new architectural publication appears, it immediately generates a mania for that particular style. When Stuart and Revett returned from Athens, and published their work on Greece, it generated a mania for Greek architecture, from which we are barely recovered. Taylor and Cresy did as much for the architecture of Rome. The travels of Belzoni and his successors produced the Egyptian Hall, and even Egyptian faced railway tunnels. The celebrated French work on the architecture of Tuscany and "Letarouilly's Modern Rome" have more recently inspired us with a desire for Italian Palaces.' Jones then talks of the elder Pugin and other architects flooding the country with Gothic buildings – using their talents 'to the reproduction of a galvanised corpse . . . from the Gothic mania we fell into the Elizabethan – a malady, fortunately, of shorter duration; for we then even worshipped not only a dead body, but a corrupt one . . . and we are even now threatened with the importation of a Renaissance mania from France'. In describing the Elizabethan style as 'corrupt' he was pointing out what was not generally recognized – that the Tudor interpretations of Renaissance detail were themselves uneducated copies of ill-digested forms, generally taken from Dutch copies of Italian books. So that the nineteenth-century revivalists were in fact taking the worst models.

This criticism, however, could hardly be levelled at Pugin or at most of the 'Goths' or, in particular, at William Burges, the greatest exponent of 'High Victorian Gothic'. Burges prepared himself for his architectural career by a lengthy Grand Tour during which he decided that classical architecture was uninteresting and thereafter devoted himself to the study of Gothic as seen in the great French cathedrals. He thoroughly absorbed and understood Gothic detail and when he came to work for the Marquess of Bute at Cardiff in the late 1860s he produced extraordinary results [pl. 170]. As well as being

169. The dining-room of Keele Hall, *c.*1870, illustrates a Victorian version of classicism where seventeenth- and eighteenth-century styles are indiscriminately mixed.

extremely competent he had a great sense of fun, which was often displayed in his use of Gothic, Arabic and Moorish detail. Burges was fortunate in his client, who understood his ideas and entered into them wholeheartedly. In the fairy-tale castle of Castel Coch, designed in the late 1870s, we have the perfect example of the romance of Victorian medievalism – the pointed turrets ascending out of a wooded hillside, the inner courtyard approached from a drawbridge, and the whole interior richly decorated with painted and stencilled walls and 'medieval' painted furniture, also designed by Burges. Castel Coch was a very rich man's plaything and Burges, rather than setting a trend, represented the marvellous late and last flowering of the Gothic revival.

It was the writings of John Ruskin that were to have the greatest effect on the theories of design and architecture in the second half of the nineteenth century [pl. 172]. Ruskin was incapable of making artistic judgements without making the equivalent moral and social ones and this alliance of artistic theory and social conscience struck a deep chord among the thinking members of the community. In 1849 he published *The Seven Lamps of Architecture*, and in 1851–3 *The Stones of Venice*; in the former he writes 'For it is not the material, but the absence of human labour, which makes the thing worthless, and a piece of terracotta, or plaster of Paris, which has been wrought by the human hand, is worth all the stone in Carrara cut by machinery.' This idea, so impossible to reconcile with a highly mechanized industrial society, was to be enthusiastically embraced by a number of writers on design – for instance Charles Eastlake, whose *Hints on Household Taste in Furniture, Upholstery and Other Details* was first published in 1868 and was in its fourth edition by 1878. This extremely practical book, if rather hectoring in tone, was written basically for women; in it the author denounces fashion and novelty in no uncertain terms – one of his favourite words is 'trash'. He also elaborates on the excellence of handwork, disapproving of perfection of finish, which together with symmetry and precision he equates with denying the human element.

Eastlake's book is basically pro-Gothic and anti-Rococo, which he calls Louis XIV style. Curved furniture and carved wood, which he castigates as 'trash', are to be substituted by his own designs. These are illustrated [pl. 173] and are vaguely Gothic or Tudor, in solid oak – veneering is 'false', as are graining and marbelizing. He also illustrates and strongly recommends a settee from Knole – this design has come to be known as a Knole sofa and has been reproduced almost without inter-

170. The nursery, Cardiff Castle, designed by William Burges, *c.*1880. In one sense the whole of Cardiff Castle is one great nursery expressing Burges's sense of fantasy and humour. Wallpaper extends from the floor to the frieze of tiles, which is painted with the figures of nursery mythology.

VALIANT TAILOR
CLEODOLINDA:
DRAGON:
ST GEORGE:
HERALD:
CINDERELLA:

171. Design for a drawing-room by B.J. Talbert, 1876. It would be hard to conceive of a more restless room. The deep frieze above the piano, derived from Jacobean and Elizabethan precedents, was a persistent feature of Victorian interiors. (Victoria and Albert Museum, London.)

172. John Ruskin's bedroom at Brantwood painted just after his death by Arthur Severn. The low-ceilinged room has no cornice and the simplest of fireplaces – the close-hung pictures provide the only decoration.

173. Charles Eastlake's design for a sideboard was illustrated in his influential book, which was first published in 1868. It shows the Victorian urge to re-create the medieval buffet in order to show off one's possessions.

ruption from that day on. Eastlake's book was extremely influential and many of his other ideas took root – for instance, his enthusiasm for oriental carpets surrounded by patterned parquet which could be bought by the yard, the use of encaustic tiles for entrance halls, simply hung curtains, and iron bedsteads. Many of these ideas were dictated by thoughts of hygiene – a matter that is dwelt upon at length by nearly all such writers at this time – and they were very many. One of the few people whose work he does wholeheartedly endorse is William Morris.

While John Ruskin's theories carried enormous weight, the designs of William Morris had at least as much impact. The public was ready for a change from the typical mid-century interior – mahogany furniture in exaggerated Rococo shapes, upholstered in strongly coloured wool, damask or horsehair and with deep buttoning and sprung seating and hung with lace antimacassars; the ubiquitous piano; huge mirrors in gilt frames; clocks and figurines under glass domes; curtains of machine-made lace framed with heavily fringed draw curtains with elaborate pelmets or lambrequins [pl. 174]. Colours were

174. The author's great aunt in the drawing-room at Shelton Oak Priory in the 1880s. The suite of 'Rococo' chairs and sofas around the fireplace was bought at the Paris Exhibition of 1855. Mirrors with various degrees of gilded composition ornament must have been produced in thousands to satisfy Victorian taste.

vivid – the first aniline dye, for purple, had been discovered in 1856 and had soon been followed by many others such as magenta, blue, aniline yellow and alizarin red, which quickly replaced madder. These were first used on woollen materials and gave a great depth and brightness of colour [pl. 176]. Pile fabrics – velvet, plush and chenille – were also much in evidence for upholstery, curtains and cloths and their deep colours added appreciably to the sombre richness of these interiors.

William Morris went up to Oxford in 1853 and there he met Edward Burne-Jones, who was to become a lifelong friend and with whom he enthusiastically studied all things medieval. It was through Burne-Jones that he met Dante Gabriel Rossetti and other members of the Pre-Raphaelite school of painters, many of whom were to work with him [pls. 175, 177]. In 1859 Morris married and set up home in the Red House designed for him by Philip Webb. It was startlingly different from cur-

175. Rossetti reading to T.W. Dunton in his sitting-room in Chelsea in 1882. The panelling of *c.*1720, would in a more important room have had raised and fielded panels (see pl. 212). Here it is painted veridian, echoed in the curtains, the rug and the upholstery of the chair and the settee. (Painting by T. Dunn, National Portrait Gallery, London.)

176. Felted material $72\frac{1}{2}$ inches (1.8m) wide – stated to have been bought at Harrods in 1868. From the textile collection at Temple Newsam.

177 (*opposite*). The highly decorated cabinet, tapestry *portière* and stained glass are all typical of the work of Burne-Jones. This painting of his dining-room also shows William Morris's rush-seated chairs and a dining-room table designed by Philip Webb.

rent architecture – the exterior was of unadorned red brick with steeply sloping roofs while the interior had open ceilings, bare floors and walls painted in medieval patterns or hung with tapestries. The stained-glass windows were by Burne-Jones and the furniture, light fittings, cutlery and glass were designed by Morris, Webb or Burne-Jones. Alfred Tennyson christened it a 'Palace of Art'. It was the difficulty of finding suitable furnishings for the Red House that made Morris determined to start manufacturing himself.

'We have no principles, no unity; the architect, the upholsterer, the paper-stainer, the weaver, the calico printer, and the potter, run each their independent course; each struggles fruitlessly, each produces in art novelty without beauty, or beauty without intelligence.' This cry from Owen Jones was exactly what Morris and his friends set about trying to improve. The firm of Morris, Marshall, Faulkner & Co., Fine Art Workmen in Painting, Carving, Furniture and the Metals was established in 1861 and continued trading, in one form or another, until 1940. The first product was a cabinet designed by Webb and painted by Morris, who drew much of his inspiration from the Renaissance collections at the Victoria and Albert Museum in London, originally formed in 1852 as the

178. The hall, 170 Queen's Gate, designed by Norman Shaw. A Queen Anne revival interior of the 1880s showing Shaw's reintroduction of bolection moulded panelling and fireplace. The quirky idea of the balcony over the fireplace was copied by Edwin Lutyens some fifteen years later.

Museum of Ornamental Art. This cabinet itself is now in the museum. Morris and Co. produced excellently designed and solidly made furniture; tapestries designed by Burne-Jones [pl. 180]; wallpaper, textiles and carpets designed by Morris himself and made using vegetable dyes and traditional methods of manufacture; and tiles designed by William de Morgan and Morris. With these standards of craftsmanship Morris created an entirely new approach to interior decoration – an approach that was to develop into the Arts and Crafts movement. This term was first employed in connection with the Combined Arts Society, whose first exhibition was held in 1888 under the chairmanship of Walter Crane. Crane, one of the artists who contributed work to 'the Firm', as it came to be called, said 'the first practical steps towards actually producing things combining use and beauty and thus enabling people so minded to deck their homes after the older and simpler English manner was taken by William Morris and his associates'.

This exactly describes the desired interior of the 'Queen Anne' style that developed around the 1870s from an interest in English vernacular architecture. Architects such as Norman Shaw were building houses that combined the use of traditional English materials – red brick, tile hanging, white painted woodwork, and sash windows – in a style that ineffectually tried to re-create the architecture of Wren [pl. 178]. The interiors were planned to give the effect of an old house with many subsequent additions – odd little rooms, cosy corners, steps up and down and bay windows with window seats. Many

179. The sitting-room in an Oxford college in the 1870s. Although the cretonne curtains match the upholstery the deep stripe of plain material links them to the door curtains. The form of the hanging shelves on either side of the mirror, the pelmet on the mantelpiece, the sloping coal box and the corner shelf are very much of the period.

of the products of the Firm were ideally suited to the Queen Anne style but, as Professor Mark Girouard has pointed out, 'it was possible for almost any art object produced during the 1870s and 1880s to be described as Queen Anne' – the term 'art objects', however, did not include buttoned Rococo furniture or the Renaissance style. The results of this eclectic buying were generally a strange cluttered mixture, the elements of which would be dependent on the taste of the owner or, more properly, the owner's wife. Colours tended to be muted in direct contrast to the brilliant artificial tones favoured by less educated members of the public. 'Art' materials from Liberty and printed cretonnes were used for upholstery and curtains. Cretonne, which was a combination of hemp, jute or linen with cotton, came into favour as a result of the cotton famine after the American Civil War of 1861. It was generally printed and was an ideal fabric for loose covers and curtains. The lack of definition of the prints in both drawing and colour owing to the coarser weave added to the appeal of a fabric that is as popular today as it was then.

Morris had been inspired by Ruskin's ideas on the intrinsic value of craftsmanship and also on the importance of beautiful surroundings in the creation of human happiness. As a lifelong socialist, it was a great disappointment to him that, despite the enormous success of his work, in the end the majority of his clients were the rich – the historic handwork methods used to produce his goods proved to be enormously expensive. However, many of his textile and wallpaper designs were to reach a much wider public – over six hundred of his completed designs are still very much in evidence today [pls. 183, 184]. Morris said, 'Whatever you have in your rooms think first of your walls, for they are that which makes your house a home.'

180. Edward Burne-Jones's design for a tapestry hanging. (Victoria and Albert Museum, London.)

181. Walter Crane's design for the wallpaper 'Swans and Rushes'. (Victoria and Albert Museum, London.)

182. Wightwick Manor. The Great Parlour was decorated *c.*1893 taking the medieval great hall as a model. Below the deep plaster frieze hangs William Morris's *Diagonal Trail* tapestry. On either side of the inglenook blue and white ware popularized by Rossetti and James McNeill Whistler is displayed on open shelves.

183. One of William Morris's designs for wallpaper.

184. The William Morris drawing for the wallpaper 'Vine' of 1873.

It could be said that his firm started a new era in the manufacture of wallpaper. The papers were actually produced by Metford Warner, who also commissioned designs from William Burges, Walter Crane, Charles Eastlake and Edward William Godwin among many others [pl. 181]. It was through Warner that wallpaper designs were first admitted as worthy of serious consideration to the London Exhibition of all Fine Arts in 1873.

Other kinds of wallpaper were also being produced – the first washable paper was made on a commercial basis as early as 1853. These papers, known as 'sanatories', were at first only self-coloured but by 1884 were multi-coloured. They remained popular until well into the twentieth century. In the 1870s a new kind of design was developed and produced by Jeffrey & Co. This combined the frieze, filling and dado, using three patterns in one overall design – a method endorsed by Charles Eastlake. In the second half of the nineteenth century it was hard to find a house with unpapered walls. During all this time traditional block and flock pattern papers of the eighteenth and early nineteenth centuries continued to be produced for the benefit of traditionalists and owners of Palladian and neoclassical houses.

Both Owen Jones and Charles Eastlake go into some detail about suitable wallpaper patterns. They both suggest diaper patterns in self tints as being 'safest' and an excellent background for pictures – a matter of some importance, as contemporary art, particularly landscapes in oil or watercolour, played an important part in decoration and was 'customary in almost every apartment'. Most drawing-rooms and dining-rooms and many bedrooms were equipped with picture rails. These were placed just under the frieze and the pictures, generally in gold mounts and frames, were hung on long wires or cords the colour of which 'should correspond with the paper or paint in the room as much as possible, so as not to be noticed'. Ideally, oil and watercolours were to be separated into different rooms and the pictures hung in one, two or three tiers,

185. Late-nineteenth-century cut velvet, 24 inches wide. The repeat is also about 24 inches. From the textile collection at Temple Newsam.

186. From *Decoration & Furniture of Town Houses* by Robert W. Edis, published in 1881, showing his own dining-room where he has designed 'a cluster of shelves specially made to take blue and white china, which, to my mind, has a much more decorative effect, arranged as I have shown, than when hung up or placed in single and isolated pieces'.

with the centre of the middle or only tier to be at eye level. As a background to pictures, Eastlake recommends 'Very light stone colour or green (not emerald) and silver-grey . . . and two shades of the same colour are generally sufficient for one paper. In drawing rooms embossed white or cream colour, with a very small diapered pattern, will not be amiss, where water colour drawings are hung.' These raised or embossed patterns became increasingly popular and by the end of the century they were being marketed by specialist firms such as Lincrusta Walton and Anaglypta, both of which became household names. For rooms hung with printed papers, Jones suggests that the prevailing colours should be green for halls and staircases, 'because most refreshing from the strong glare of daylight' and dull reds in diapers or flock for studies and dining-rooms, while drawing-rooms 'where the paper has to do more towards furnishing and beautifying a room, they may be more gay; almost any tone or shade of colour heightened with gold may be used'.

In 1862, only a year after the establishment of William Morris's firm, the International Exhibition included a section of arts and crafts from Japan. After years of isolation the art of Japan was practically unknown in England and the Japanese stands at this exhibition excited great interest not least in E.W. Godwin, who, in common with Rossetti and Whistler, was buying Japanese prints. He was also decorating his house in Bristol in the Japanese style with plain walls hung with Japanese prints and blue and white oriental porcelain – this at almost exactly the same time as Philip Webb was designing the Red House for Morris. Godwin became the great designer in the 'Japanese' style, which was to lead to the 'aesthetic movement' – characterized by rather austere interiors with blue and white porcelain, Japanese screens, peacock feathers, matting, wicker and bamboo furniture and Japanese artefacts. Another enthusiast for the Japanese style was young Arthur Liberty, who became the manager of the oriental department of Farmer and Rogers's Great Shawl & Cloak Emporium after he had persuaded them to buy all the available Japanese goods from the 1862 exhibition. After thirteen years he opened his own shop, Liberty's in Regent Street – a name that was to become synonymous with the 'aesthetic movement'. It was here that 'art' furniture, carpets, curtains, Moorish tables, brass trays and bric-a-brac could be bought at reasonable prices. He also commissioned designs for textiles, and 'Liberty prints' have been famous from that day to this.

The fashion for collecting blue and white china became as much of a mania as it had been in the late seventeenth century; the way of displaying it, however, was not so happy [pl. 186]. The taste for 'Japonaiserie' and the 'aesthetic movement' was all-pervasive and in the latter part of the century there was scarcely an interior that did not reflect in some way, however minor, these influences [pl. 188]. Godwin, for instance, was by the 1870s, designing wallpaper in the 'Japanese' style, incorporating motifs such as fans and 'pies'. These latter roundels or discs were derived from patterns on Japanese blue and white porcelain and were used indiscriminately by English architects and designers in decoration of every kind.

Unfortunately, in lesser hands the 'aesthetic' interior could be a gloomy disaster. This admiring description from the *Paper Hanger and Decorator's Assistant* of 1879 is fairly typical: 'the dining room . . . walls are a dark drab, with a high dado of mauve and drab in alternate bands, and a frieze of sober-hued stamped leather . . . the fireplace, over which is a mantelpiece of oak and walnut, with ebonized mouldings, in the centre of

187. The vogue for French furniture is shown in this late-nineteenth-century painting of a comfortable but grand London drawing-room. Shoulder-height glass draught screens figure largely in this type of decoration.

which is fixed a life size marble medallion . . . opposite to this stands a high oaken sideboard with mirror, and above this a shelf for china, and above that again a curved recess covered with stamped leather . . . the curtain that divides the dining room from the antechamber . . . is the work of the lady of the house [and] quite perfect as a work of art. In colour it is a dark bluish-green, and it is crossed by broad bands of pale yellow, and black velvet, beneath which are embroidered at intervals circular devices of peacock's feathers. These, with the rare blue china, the Salviata vases, the choice brass-work and bronzes, and other 'objets d'art' sprinkled about, serve as points of positive colour, to brighten up the room.' The same author notes, 'It is indeed surprising how widespread is the demand for aesthetic decoration. That which but a few years ago was reserved for princes or rich magnates . . . may be said to be now within the reach of all. We have gone from one extreme to the other. House decoration is quite the rage.'

The mention of the curtain dividing the room from the antechamber and the fact that it is the work of the lady of the house is quite significant. *Portières*, or heavy room-dividing curtains, had been in fashion since the 1850s and were strongly recommended by Eastlake in his *Hints on Household Taste* – hangings, also, had been revived by William Morris in the form not only of tapestries, but also of embroidered cloths worked by amateurs but designed by Morris and his associates. The extraordinary amount of hand- and needlework undertaken by women in the nineteenth century gave an outlet for artistic expression and added an individual touch to decoration in the shape of embroidered cushions, bed covers, table covers and almost every object that could, conceivably, be embellished with needlework.

The 'aesthetic movement' attracted almost as much satire as admiration. In 1881 Gilbert and Sullivan wrote an entire opera, *Patience*, on this theme. A few of the lines give something of the flavour:

> Though the Philistines may jostle,
> you will rank as an apostle
> in the high aesthetic band,
> If you walk down Piccadilly
> with a poppy or a lily
> in your medieval hand.

and:

> A greenery-yallery, Grosvenor Gallery,
> Foot-in-the-grave young man!

188. *Summer* by Atkinson Grimshaw shows the Japanese influence as expressed in an upper-middle-class household, with fans above the door, thin mats on the floor and blue and white porcelain which also looks convincing with the seventeenth-century-style Dutch furniture.

Despite the movement towards the 'aesthetic' interior, rich and aristocratic society continued to favour the 'French' [pl. 187] or 'Italianate' styles that had found expression from the 1830s to the 1850s in the refurbishment of many of the great London houses such as Stafford House and Devonshire House. The magnificent series of rooms in the Louis XV style in Stafford House [pl. 190], created in the 1830s, set a pattern of decoration for grand London interiors that endured until 1914. The William Kent saloon in Devonshire House was redecorated in the 1840s in the Italianate manner and at Grosvenor House the state rooms were remodelled in the 1870s in Italian Renaissance style by the first Duke of Westminster.

The Italianate style had been given royal approval with the rebuilding of Osborne House in the 1840s for Queen Victoria

189. The gold-starred paper of this mid-Victorian boudoir is echoed in the deep cove by a similar paper with closer set stars. The white and gold theme is continued in the white marble fireplace and gilded mirror and picture frames. The porcelain plates, mounted on velvet and framed in gilt wood, are a special feature.

190. A painting of 1848 of the gallery at Stafford House (now Lancaster House). It was originally designed by Wyatt for the Duke of York but became the home of the 2nd Duke of Sutherland, who then employed Charles Barry. It was to the Duchess that Queen Victoria remarked on her first visit to Stafford House 'I have come from my house to your palace'.

and Prince Albert. Other houses were built in this style at intervals during the nineteenth century – generally furnished with sumptuous 'Renaissance' textiles and furniture. Italy, in particular Venice, was a happy hunting ground for 'antique' furniture, objects, hangings and pictures, and for those who could not afford the time or who did not quite trust their own taste and judgement there were plenty of antique dealers ready to supply 'authentic' goods from Italian *palazzi*.

All these different styles of decoration current in the second half of the nineteenth century, from the humblest to the grandest, had one thing in common – namely, the crowding of more and more furniture and objects into each room [pl. 191]. Even 'aesthetic' interiors in the Japanese style were overlaid with a plethora of fans, samurai swords, shawls, and lacquer boxes. The enormous increase in mass production of furniture, textiles and wallpaper meant that individuality had to be expressed not only by the arrangement and choice of such things, but also by the addition of a multitude of knick-knacks and objects, resulting in the extraordinarily cluttered interiors associated with this period.

191. The hall and staircase of a country house, painted by Jonathon Pratt in 1882. The almost photographic quality of the picture gives confidence in its veracity and the great jumble of objects, in particular the sporting trophies, muddled about on every surface is typical of the 'non-decoration' of such a house.

9

THE SEARCH FOR SIMPLICITY

'It was as if Spring had come all of a sudden.' This comment by the Belgian designer Henri Van der Velde referred to wallpapers designed by Charles Annesley Voysey. It might with reason have been said of his work in general. In 1883 Voysey sold his first wallpaper to Jeffrey & Co., thereafter he produced countless designs for wallpaper, fabrics, carpets [pl. 193] and furniture as well as designing a number of unpretentious houses, the interiors of which must, at the time, have seemed shockingly simple and direct. In its freshness and lightness Voysey's work had no parallel outside the pages of children's books illustrated by Kate Greenaway and others.

Twenty-six years younger than Norman Shaw and twelve years older than Edwin Lutyens, he displayed no signs of their eclectic propensities, remaining obstinately bound by his own integrity and almost certainly oblivious of his influence on the later development of the 'Modern' style, which he came to despise. Although grounded in the vernacular tradition Voysey's work appears unencumbered by the dead weight of the past that still affected his contemporaries. His interiors are free of clutter, sparse in architectural detail and largely devoid of any individual mannerisms. This unpretentious simplicity together with the long, horizontal windows, low ceilings and white walls of his rooms give them a remarkably modern appearance [pl. 192].

In almost all interiors at the turn of the century, a lack of repose was just as evident as it had been in the preceding fifty years. But repose was a quality that Voysey prized, sought and achieved. It may seem strange that Voysey, perhaps the most successful wallpaper and textile designer of his time, seldom used the designs in his own interiors, but he makes his reasons clear: 'We cannot be too simple . . . we are too apt to furnish our rooms as if we regarded our wallpapers, furniture and fabrics as far more attractive than our friends'. Voysey is vehement in his condemnation of decorative trappings: 'Instead of painting boughs of apple trees on our door panels and covering every shelf with petticoats of silk, let us begin by discarding the mass of useless ornaments and banishing the millinery that degrades our furniture and fittings. Reduce the variety of colours and patterns in a room.' This exhortation was quoted in the first number of *The Studio*, which was published in 1893 and was the most influential and successful of the magazines at that time devoted to the decorative arts.

In championing Voysey and the architect Baillie Scott, *The Studio* gave prominence to the Arts and Crafts movement. While very much part of that movement, Voysey's visual puritanism drove him beyond its rather parochial confines. Baillie Scott's interiors were more characteristic of Arts and Crafts principles and altogether much less austere than Voysey's. Like William Morris before him, Baillie Scott was glancing over his shoulder – the lure of medieval England was still a potent force. Half-timbered walls and Gothic allusions are recurrent themes in his rooms, and the halls of his small houses or large cottages sometimes assume medieval pretensions as multi-purpose rooms in miniature [pl. 194].

No feature of Arts and Crafts interiors encapsulates the essence of the movement more perfectly than the inglenook. The 'womb chamber' provided the ultimate safe and warm escape from the harsh realities of the world. In the 1880s Norman Shaw had created an inglenook in the drawing-room at Cragside with 10 tons of elaborately carved Italian marble embracing leather-covered settees on either side of the fireplace. The more humble versions by Baillie Scott and other Arts and Crafts designers provided an opportunity to display hand-made tiles; and for the less ostentatious – and much less comfortable – seating arrangements they designed oak benches which were made like other furniture for their rooms by the

Guild of Handicrafts or one of the other guilds which were formed at this time.

The very word guild had suitably medieval connotations but these new versions were not set up to protect a particular trade but to promote a group of artists and craftsmen whose work encompassed a wide range of different crafts from furniture and fabrics to metalwork and jewellery. A.H. Mackmurdo founded the Century Guild in 1882 and six years later another architect, Charles Ashbee, founded the Guild and School of Handicraft. But during the first decade of the twentieth century it became clear that the whole philosophy of such enterprises could not be sustained indefinitely however committed the participants remained – even Ashbee admitted in 1910 that 'modern civilisation rests on machinery, and no system for the

192. The hall in Voysey's own house The Orchard, designed in 1899, shows the freshness and simplicity he achieved. Apart from the ironmongery and the picture rail this interior looks forward to the mid-1920s despite the fact that the wall below the picture rail was originally painted a dark colour.

encouragement or the endowment of the teaching of the arts can be sound that does not recognise this'.

Mackmurdo's influence extended to another style with his title page for the book *Wren's City Churches*. When it was published in 1883 it was the earliest example of Art Nouveau design – a style that flourished on the Continent but made little impact in England. Art Nouveau was born out of the Arts and Crafts movement, with a strong infusion of Japonaiserie from the 'aesthetic' style, to which were added the asymmetrical curves of Rococo and later the influence of Celtic art. All these constituents were combined to produce the sinuous and extenuated curves of natural foliage, which were progressively exaggerated and finally abstracted. Art Nouveau derived its name from a Parisian shop; in Italy it was known as *Stile Liberty* after the London shop.

In England Art Nouveau was considered decadent, and as if to underline its unimportance it was frequently referred to by the epithet 'quaint'. It only gained acceptance as a style in designs for textiles, wallpaper and metalwork, and more particularly in jewellery, all of which were promoted in *The Studio* magazine and designed by concerns such as Arthur Silver's Silver Studio and the Guilds. Although Voysey himself

193. Wallpaper design by Charles Annesley Voysey entitled 'Let us Prey' – it seems appropriate for a nursery as do many of the designs by Voysey and his contemporaries. (Victoria and Albert Museum, London.)

194. In this scheme of 1906 for a dining-room, M.H. Baillie Scott has worked Art Nouveau decoration into an otherwise 'cottagey' interior. The 'built-in' furniture and inglenook are typical of the period. The complexity of the decoration in this room should be compared with Voysey's room in Plate 192.

remained largely unaffected by the style, some of his designs for wallpaper and textiles were an inspiration for designers on the Continent. Only in Scotland in and around Glasgow did the style gain any wider acceptance – in the work of Charles Rennie Mackintosh, his wife Margaret Macdonald and the 'Glasgow School'. But their buildings and interiors made little impact on Scotland south of the border, although their influence on European designers was considerable. In transcending the ephemeral and purely decorative nature of Art Nouveau, Mackintosh became an important precursor of the Modern Movement.

It is ironic that having plundered Europe for ideas for eight hundred years, in the second half of the nineteenth century the British made three highly important contributions to the Modern Movement – Paxton's iron and glass envelope for the Great Exhibition and the Arts and Crafts and Art Nouveau movements – and then left their development to designers on the Continent while those in England reverted, once again, to looking backwards.

Once manufacturers had begun to produce cheap and often debased copies of Arts and Crafts and Art Nouveau designs these inevitably lost their appeal for the section of rich middle-class society that had been able to afford the hand-crafted work of the guilds. As Arts and Crafts products drifted down market after World War I and Art Nouveau descended into the bathos of Art Deco they found their home in the thousands of equally adulterated versions of Voysey's original houses in the new suburbs [pl. 195]. At the same time other manufacturers were at work turning out reproduction Hepplewhite and Sheraton

195. Arts and Crafts interior from Edward Gregory's *Art and Craft of Homemaking* (1915). By 1925 when the second edition was published the Arts and Crafts movement had descended in the social scale. The inappropriately large frieze and cornice provide the only purely decorative touches. Window-length curtains are now the norm.

196. Adam revival design by the firm of Crace and Son, *c.*1880. From 1788 successive members of the family worked on Carlton House, the Brighton Pavilion and with Pugin on the Houses of Parliament. They remained one of the most successful firms in decoration and furniture-making throughout the nineteenth century.

to satisfy the increasing demand for suitable furniture to complement the new Adam revival interiors [pl. 196].

Most Adam revival rooms would have been unrecognizable to Robert Adam himself. His neo-classical details were arranged in an arbitrary and haphazard manner often combined incongruously with adaptations of various elements borrowed from both Louis XV and Louis XVI decoration [pl. 197]. The somewhat bizarre results were, however, recognizably classical and the emergence of this decorative style around 1880 marked the end of the Victorian taste for Tudor and Gothic as a fashionable architectural style for important new houses. At a less exalted level of society speculative builders were still building terraces of Italianate houses which, while they may not have satisfied Victorian ideals of individualism, certainly made economic sense. The sash window was an important feature of these Italianate houses, each sash being fitted with a single sheet of plate glass. In the Queen Anne revival the sash window reverted to the eighteenth-century pattern with glazing bars, so that by the time the Adam style became fashionable this one element had already made its reappearance. Superficially this might have seemed an unimportant detail but it was one indication of a decisive change in attitude to the interpretation of past styles. In the 1870s a few people began to show an interest in eighteenth-century portraits and furniture and ten years later this was expanded to include a much more accurate observation of classical interiors. This historical approach, incidentally despised by the followers of Art Nouveau, gained ground in the 1890s when both the *Architectural Review* and *Country Life* were founded. Both magazines promoted this new scholarly interest, with the result that Edwardian interiors present an altogether more authentic interpretation of eighteenth-century models than the Victorians' earlier attempts. A number of books published at this time underline the scholarship that was being directed at past styles of architecture and decoration, and the gathering interest in these subjects added further impetus to the restoration of old houses – a cause that William Morris had first espoused when he founded the Society for the Protection of Ancient Buildings in 1877 [pl. 198].

Whether restoring old houses or building new ones, owners were anxious to take advantage of anything that might add to their comfort although few matched the American father of the future Countess of Craven of whom it was said: 'Where other fathers placed a pearl necklace, Mr Bradley Martin

197. Gillow design for an 'Adam style' Octagon Boudoir at the Paris Exposition 1878. The 'panels hung with blue figured satin divided by pilasters decorated in shades of blue and gold on maize-coloured silk, the general tone of the ceiling being ivory colour, with the background of the enrichments lightly tinted in green'.

placed an elevator'.

Gas fires were introduced about 1880 and electric fires ten years later, but much more important was the invention, during the 1880s, of the incandescent electric bulb and the incandescent mantle for gaslight. At last an efficient and, more particularly, a clean source of artificial light was available, if only for a limited number of households – even by 1919 only 6% of houses had electricity. For the fortunate it added one more dimension to the general cause of lightening the gloom associated with most late-Victorian interiors.

One further aspect of the general air of lightness in Edwardian interiors was the removal of Victorian clutter. We have already given Voysey's emphatic views on the subject but the new historicism had the same effect when the plethora of Victorian furniture was banished to the attics in favour of genuine furniture 'in period' with its surroundings. Although the exceptionally comfortable sofas and armchairs, so characteristic of the hedonism of the rich at this time, were often retained, their loose covers were invariably of flowered chintz or cretonne with pale-coloured or off-white grounds. The

198. The Green Room, Kelmscott Manor. William Morris and Rossetti took out a joint tenancy of this Elizabethan house in 1871. The room is hung with 'Kennet', one of Morris's most successful chintzes, in graduated tones of indigo with touches of yellow and green.

199. The self-taught artist and craftsman, Frank Dickinson, a follower of Morris and Ruskin designed and built Little Holland House and its furniture and fittings in 1903. The sitting-room in the house exemplifies both the spartan degree of comfort and the hand-crafted ornament, such as the tiles and the beaten copper in the fireplace surround, associated with the Arts and Crafts interiors.

heavy curtaining associated with late Victorian times was discarded in favour of less elaborate arrangements more suited to the rest of the decoration, and *portières* disappeared. Silk seems to have been one of the most popular materials and grey, grey green and grey blue among the more favoured colours. It was at this time that Robert Adam's name was brought into the colour spectrum – Adam greens and blues proliferating on walls everywhere both in the relatively new mansion flats as well as in country houses. They bore little relation to Adam's clean sharp colours, the originals of which had been subjected to well over a century of coal fires. As a result the walls as well as the silk curtains had a slightly dusty hue.

The general drive for simpler and lighter interiors made consistent if somewhat slow progress from the 1870s on and was evident in both principal types of decoration – that of the Arts and Crafts movement, where the cottagey interiors display a visible, even moralistic, lack of comfort [pl. 199]; and that of the rich Edwardian Adam style town and country houses

200. Edwin Lutyens designed The Deanery for Edward Hudson, the founder and proprietor of *Country Life* magazine, in 1899–1900. Here Lutyens brought the Arts and Crafts style to its height. The profusion of dowels in the woodwork is a typical Lutyens trick in his interiors of this period.

which flaunt comfort [pl. 201]. This progress might have continued to its logical conclusion after World War I had the Modern Movement or International style become acceptable outside a limited group of people very often drawn from the same *avant-garde* section of society whose predecessors had patronized the Arts and Crafts movement [pl. 200].

The first house built in England in the International style was appropriately enough designed by a German architect, Peter Behrens, in 1925 for the engineer W.J. Basset-Lowke. Not unexpectedly perhaps, the *avant-garde* Mr Basset-Lowke had some nine years before provided Charles Rennie Mackintosh with his only realized commission south of the border – the remodelling of his house in Northampton.

The Canadian architect Wells Coates, who had settled in England in the 1920s, founded the Mars (Modern Architectural Research) Group and the cause was strengthened in the thirties when a number of distinguished refugees from Hitler's Germany arrived in England, among them Walter Gropius who, as head of the Bauhaus in Germany, had formulated and taught the philosophy of the Modern Movement. Sadly World War II allowed no time for architects and designers to establish any continuity in the development of the style. Even after the war it never regained the necessary momentum to break down the resistance of a people conditioned by endemic nostalgia.

In sixty years only a minute proportion of clients in England commissioned houses in the International style and of those the best are often the ones that architects designed for them-

selves, such as Serge Chermayeff's house at Halland, which he designed in 1934 [pl. 203]. Bereft of commissions, a number of these Continental architects, Chermayeff and Gropius among them, left for America. Of their English colleagues a few like Oliver Hill found sympathetic and rich patrons [pl. 202]. Others provided modern interiors within a vernacu-

201. Walter Brierley's design for the dining-room (now a kitchen) at Normanby Park, part of his alterations to the house in 1905–7, shows an Edwardian classical grandeur owing something to late-seventeenth-century interiors in the ceiling and bolection moulded panelling and also to early-eighteenth-century Baroque designs in the use of pilasters.

202. Dining-room at Jolwynds designed by Oliver Hill in 1930. An all-white room with chairs upholstered in white calf. The only concession to architectural detail was confined to the service end of the room, where he provided a twentieth-century version of William Kent's dining-room at Houghton (see pl. 77).

lar shell for patrons who were not wholly committed to the International style. In many such cases the clients' wish to incorporate antique furniture in their new rooms presented a problem that was never really satisfactorily solved. Eighteenth-century furniture in particular is not seen to best advantage in rooms with large expanses of white wall and plate glass.

Apart from white ceilings and walls, simplicity was maintained by omitting cornices or restricting them to simple coves and eliminating architectural details wherever practicable [pl. 204]. Natural wood was commonly used for the floors of halls and sitting-rooms, on which a rug by a fashionable designer such as the American Marion Dorn would sometimes

be the only concession to decorative treatment. Fitted carpets in plain colours became and have remained a standard floor covering for bedrooms in every style of decoration.

Marion Dorn, who was working in England during the twenties and thirties, produced geometric patterns for curtain and upholstery material as well as for carpets, although she also used stylized versions of natural forms. Other designs were produced by artists such as Duncan Grant and Vanessa Bell both of whom had been associated with the Bloomsbury offshoot – Roger Fry's ill-fated Omega Workshop, inspired by William Morris, which closed down in 1920 after only seven years, the result of Fry's lack of business acumen as much as of World War I. Stylized natural forms such as leaves, flowers or birds were often used singly or grouped in isolation from each other, making use of only two or three colours, unlike traditional designs where the pattern was more or less continuous and the colours less limited. Many of these designs were printed by means of commercial hand screening in the 1930s, which was one of a number of techniques introduced at this time. Others included the use of chemical dyes, which preven-

203. Serge Chermayeff's own house was only built after long planning delays, *c.*1938. It is doubtful whether any house in England built in the succeeding fifty years has surpassed it as an example of the International style. Note the absence of decoration and the extension of the terrace into the living room.

ted colours from 'flying' or fading from sunlight or washing, and chemical treatments to prevent shrinkage.

As natural fibres became increasingly expensive, new man-made fibres were produced, the most successful being rayon, which could be used with natural fibres to create different effects but was also used on its own from the late twenties. For those who did not want the sheen of rayon, the manufacturers used slubbed yarns that gave the appearance of 'shabbiness', while the use of irregular yarns simulated the hand-made look. Even tapestry was being machine made in the twenties and thirties; at the same time manufacturers did not neglect traditional chintzes and cretonnes, which were in demand for all those decorating in the historical taste.

Built-in furniture had appeared before the end of the nineteenth century, but it had always been treated as an elaborate decorative element and even the simpler Arts and Crafts or Art Nouveau versions had been used as a vehicle for displaying specially designed ironwork hinges and handles. In modern interiors built-in furniture was often completely devoid of ornament. Any decorative intent was confined to the use of natural wood as a material for the flush doors and drawers. But most built-in furniture was simply painted white, and its rounded corners and strong horizontal emphasis showed the twenties' and thirties' preoccupation with 'streamline modern', which was associated in people's minds with the excitement of speed and aerodynamics [pl. 205].

204. Living room at Ashcombe Tower designed by Brian O'Rorke in the mid-1930s. Despite the sash windows and minor decorative details like the fireplace surround, the room has the trappings of advanced 1930s taste - white walls and curtains, rugs and chairs designed by the American designer Marion Dorn.

205. Marion Dorn's own sitting-room, 1938. Marion Dorn used her own fabrics in this redecoration of an existing flat in Chelsea. The strong horizontal emphasis is used to counteract the unfashionable height of the room. The lower bookcase, curved banquette and table are typical of this particular style.

Mirror glass was used in large sheets both for decorative effect and to give the illusion of space in rooms that were increasingly subject to economic considerations and therefore smaller than their Victorian and Edwardian counterparts [pl. 206]. Precisely because the International style eschewed decoration in general and ornament in particular it had little appeal for the rich and fashionable, although the successful decorator Syrie Maugham abstracted various ideas and reworked them into her schemes.

Mrs Maugham made extensive use of mirrors and white in various tones – white walls, upholstery, curtains and even furniture provided a suitably modern and stylish setting for her chic and wealthy clients. She used mirror plate for fireplace surrounds, picture frames, table tops and screens as well as setting it in panels or covering whole walls with it. She also used mirrors conventionally, not surprisingly preferring the Venetian variety with mirrored frames. The success of her glamorous and sophisticated rooms was matched and perhaps boosted by the lavish display of the same ingredients in the film sets devised by Van Nest Polglase and his designers for the Fred Astaire and Ginger Rogers movies [pl. 207].

Syrie Maugham not only painted furniture white she also stripped antique furniture of its paint. The famous American decorator Elsie de Wolff is reputed to have made the waspish comment that 'one day darling Syrie will arrange to be pickled in her own coffin'. The pickling of antiques in tanks of acid was not confined to furniture or to Mrs Maugham. In the thirties there was also a vogue for stripping old pine panelling and staircases, despite the fact that cheap pine was originally used only because its coarse grain was destined to be hidden by paint. It is a practice that still has many adherents.

Although Syrie Maugham was the most famous of the lady decorators she was not the first. Rhoda and Agnes Garrett had published *Suggestions for House Decoration in Painting, Woodwork and Furniture* as early as 1879. They were followed by Miss 'Bunch' Frith, daughter of the painter W.P. Frith, who was decorating in a restrained classical taste during the first two decades of the twentieth century. Mrs Maugham extended her practice to the United States and in this she was reversing a general trend. While few American decorators or designers worked in England their influence was certainly apparent. American heiresses provided both the impetus and the money for the decoration of just the kind of houses that had so impressed their fellow countryman Henry James after he had settled in England in 1876. Other Americans such as the Astors bought

large houses in England and, on a less opulent scale, yet others such as Edward Knoblock brought a detailed knowledge of architecture and decoration and infused the English scene with an American sense of style, particularly in the arrangement of rooms.

The Americans also understood the importance of comfort particularly in regard to heating. Although the Duke of Wellington had installed a hot water central heating system at Stratfield Saye as early as 1833 it was, like many systems at the time, prone to overheating. It was not until the last two decades of the nineteenth century that many of the problems were overcome and it became practical to install central heating in private houses. Even then there remained the problem of concealing the bulky and unsightly radiators, which was only solved by hiding them behind grills ingeniously designed to match the decoration but inevitably adding to the cost of this already expensive luxury. Central heating systems, like bathrooms, were to be found only in the houses of the rich.

206. The potential for glamorizing bathrooms was discovered in the 1930s, largely through the Hollywood movies; fortunately there were still servants to keep the large expanses of mirror glass in pristine condition. This example was designed for a London flat by Syrie Maugham in 1937.

207. The drawing-room in Syrie Maugham's own house in the Kings Road, Chelsea, *c.* 1930, displays her sense of chic. The tall screen is in mirror glass and the low one in white lacquer, the two-tone cream rug is by Marion Dorn and the long sofas are upholstered in beige satin.

It is somewhat surprising to discover that between 1880 and 1910 the best bathrooms in the world were in England. The individually made porcelain bath tubs and basins and ceramic tiles provided a new opportunity for decoration, and catalogues of the time show intriguing designs for Tudor and other styles applied to bath panels.

At this level of luxurious extravagance the simplicity that was becoming more and more apparent elsewhere held no allure for the owners of large and grand Edwardian houses, who continued to have their rooms decorated either in a Renaissance style or in the still popular French Rococo taste. In choosing Rococo there was sometimes the advantage of being able to use eighteenth-century panelling that had been removed from a French château, as William Waldorf Astor did at Cliveden, where he installed the elegant *boiseries* from the Château d'Asnieres in his dining-room. Such instances were few and demonstrated a lack of interest in the new trends that people like Edward Knoblock were setting. When Knoblock moved to London from Paris in 1914, his appreciation of the French Empire and *Directoire* styles was matched by a natural interest in the English equivalent, and the Regency interiors that he created both in London and in Sussex mark the beginning of a Regency revival [pl. 209]. Fortunately for him his inauguration of what he called 'solemn Regency' coincided with the important sale at the Deepdene of Thomas Hope's furniture in 1917.

In adding Regency to the spectrum of acceptable classical styles Edward Knoblock was unknowingly laying some of the foundations for what was to become the most fashionable style of decoration in the second half of the twentieth century – known now as the 'country house look'. Although Knoblock and later the architect Lord Gerald Wellesley among others decorated their houses in a more or less pure version of one aspect of Regency taste, interest in a less solemn and grand vein of the Regency was centring on Soane's interiors rather than Hope's and on the painted furniture rather than the rosewood of the period. As a result of mixing dissimilar types of furniture of the same period in one room the eye became accustomed to such juxtapositions and the idea of furnishing rooms strictly 'in period' gradually lost its appeal. If the decoration and furnishing of rooms just before World War II and after demonstrated a marked preference for the eighteenth and early nineteenth century, at least this provided a very broad base from which to work.

In the 1920s a number of people oblivious as yet to the charm

208. Rex Whistler's *trompe-l'œil* painting of the drapery in this room should be compared with Chippendale's carved and painted pelmets at Harewood (pl. 113) and this tent room with a real tent room (pls. 132, 133). Oliver Hill has suggested that Whistler may have developed his technique from scenic wallpapers.

of the Regency and perhaps bored by the popularity of the Adam style began to look at earlier eighteenth-century models. This trend was epitomized at the highest level by the future Lord and Lady Cholmondeley's decision to live in and restore Houghton Hall [pls. 70, 77], which they had been given as a wedding present and which had come to the family through marriage with the Walpoles. The restoration of Houghton brought William Kent's decoration and Palladian architecture into its important place in early twentieth-century taste, where it has remained.

One person who was drawn to English Palladianism was the painter Rex Whistler, who in 1930 received one of his earliest commissions, from Lady Cholmondeley's brother Sir Philip Sassoon – to paint the tent room at Port Lympne [pl. 208]. Later a number of other artists, notably Martin Battersby, revived the art of *trompe-l'œil* mural painting but its appeal seems to have been sporadic. Baroque buildings appear in a number of Rex Whistler's murals and give a hint of the revival of interest in this style in the thirties, which extended the choice of classical styles yet further back – to the seventeenth century. Although very few rooms of the period were decorated in the Baroque taste, rather more had Rococo features, in particular those rooms designed by Felix Harbord where he employed Italian plasterers to carry out his designs in stucco.

209. Regency revival in the drawing-room of Edward Knoblock's house in Worthing, *c.* 1919. The French scenic wallpaper (possibly by Jourdan & Villard) was cut up to form panels as there was not enough to paper the whole room. Early-nineteenth-century scenic papers were far more popular in France and America than in England, possibly because the paintings that the English had amassed on their Grand Tours needed the wall space.

While magazines like *Vogue* and *House and Garden* featured each new fashionable aspect of decoration the many books published by authors such as Margaret Jourdain and Professor Albert Richardson and the weekly articles in *Country Life* by Christopher Hussey and Arthur Oswald brought a new and infinitely more scholarly approach to domestic architecture and furnishing. That this approach and the interest in the subject it aroused should have been directed to such an overwhelming extent to the country house was hardly surprising since these houses provided not only a vast source of relevant information but a tantalizing insight into what many regarded as an ideal way of life in the most glamorous of surroundings.

210. Mrs Nancy Lancaster, with John Fowler, restored and decorated the derelict Haseley Court in 1955–8. The saloon is lined with aquamarine silk and the furnishing is deliberately varied from the mid-eighteenth-century Rococo girandoles to the Victorian 'conversational'. The curtaining of the central window is an example of Fowler's elaborate drapery.

In the years immediately after World War II most people who had enjoyed that life, and many who simply wished they had, feared the worst but they failed to take into account the power that nostalgia would exert once conditions improved. Many gave up the struggle but more set about bringing their houses sufficiently up to date and manageable enough to be lived in in a world without servants. This usually involved alterations, frequently extensive ones which in turn meant redecorating. Of the professional decorators who had been working in the pre-war years, Ronald Fleming, Alexis French and Felix Harbord were among the most successful, but after the war it was to the Brook Street establishment of Colefax and Fowler that an increasing number of people turned for advice. John Fowler joined Lady Colefax in 1937 and he has proved to be the most influential decorator of the second half of the century. He also established the 'country house look' as one of the most important and long-lasting styles of twentieth-century decoration.

After the war Mrs Lancaster bought Colefax and Fowler. She only collaborated with John Fowler on the decoration of her own houses or apartments. The results [pls. 210, 211] demonstrate the particular blend of elegance and comfort that was evident in so much of Fowler's work at the height of his career in the fifties and sixties. In the two decades before the war Nancy Lancaster, then married to the Anglo-American Ronald Tree, had been involved in the decoration of two houses designed by James Gibbs in the early eighteenth century – Kelmarsh, which the Trees rented, and the much grander Ditchley Park, which they bought. At Kelmarsh she was helped by Mrs Guy Bethell, among others, who was one of the most respected decorators of that period, while at Ditchley the Trees employed the French decorator Stephane Boudin. Between them they made Ditchley into probably the most comfortable house in England as well as one of the most spectacular. Nancy Lancaster has always dismissed the idea that she had any influence on John Fowler; he, on the other hand, told us many years ago that in two particular areas her influence was considerable – that of extreme comfort, which should never give the appearance of luxury; and a proper sense of scale, where overscaling is not merely preferable to underscaling but sometimes desirable.

Regardless of the importance of the house John Fowler was working on, his research, painstaking attention to architectural detail, and his unrivalled sense and fearless use of colour were all apparent, as was his ability to create in a progression

211. In Mrs Lancaster's London apartment she and John Fowler used a highly glazed finish on the bright yellow walls and they marbelized the cornice. Originally every book in the painted bookcases was provided with a special sharp pink dust cover. One armchair is deliberately upholstered in a different material to the sofa and second chair.

through his rooms a feeling of comfortable surprise. His knowledge of materials and historically correct methods of upholstery gave him the freedom to produce magnificent and elaborate designs for curtains that had not been seen since the Regency. He often used the expression 'humble elegance' in connection with his work but this only really applied to his own houses and a very limited number of his commissions [pl. 212]. It has been left to others to try to emulate him in this respect, both in Britain.and in the United States.

* * *

John Fowler retired in 1969 but just before this he had been asked by the National Trust to advise on the redecoration of some of their houses – in particular Clandon Park. This was a new departure which proved the important position in which historical decoration was now regarded. Fowler continued as the Trust's advisor on decoration until his death in 1977, when David Mlinaric was appointed to succeed him. The growth of the National Trust (now nearly two million members) and the steady increase since World War II in the number of houses open to the public has made it possible for a very large number of people to gain an insight into the decorative styles of the past. As a result the appeal of the country house is stronger than ever and a very widespread interest in interior decoration in general has developed, fostered by the large number of books, magazines and articles devoted to the subject.

There has also been a considerable increase in the number of professional decorators, a large number of whom are providing the country house look for their clients. Others have broadened the historical approach to include interpretations of Victorian, Edwardian and Art Deco decoration. Yet others such as David Hicks, who had begun to work in a contemporary style by the early 1960s, sought to provide an alternative to the various historical styles. But while as a nation we seem happy to accept contemporary decoration in offices, restaurants and shops, the resistance against modern interiors in houses appears to be as strong as ever. Even the current fashion for post-Modernism with its 'decorative' allusions to past styles is little more than an attempt to have it both ways – yet one more instance of the lure of the past which has been such a pervasive theme in this history.

212. Strawberry House, the authors' own house in London, was decorated by John Fowler in 1951 and is a rare example of Fowler's 'humble elegance'. The early-eighteenth-century fielded panelling and cornice were 'dragged' in distemper in two tones of grey and a 'dirty' white. The French headed raw silk curtains were dyed in one of Fowler's favourite sharp yellows.

GLOSSARY

Architrave The third and lowest division of the *entablature* beneath the *cornice* and *frieze*. The term is also applied to the moulding round doors and windows.

Blue paper 'The Blue Paper Warehouse' was established in the 1690s and offered different kinds of paper. There are numerous references to 'blue paper' which, due to the availability of indigo, must have been one of the cheapest coloured papers. Also, blue is a natural deterrent to flies.

Caffoy As with most 'historic' names for textiles, an inexact term. Generally understood in the eighteenth century to refer to a wool pile fabric imitating silk damask or velvet.

Capital The decorated head of a column.

Coffering Ceiling decoration consisting of recessed square or polygonal panels, usually with decorative motifs in the centre.

Cornice The projecting top section of an *entablature*. Also the top moulding on walls, interior or exterior.

Coromandel lacquer Lacquer that is laid on in a series of colours and then incised to show these.

Coved ceiling The concave area between a wall and the flat bed of the ceiling.

Crewel work Embroidery, generally on plain linen or wool, using two-ply worsted yarn.

Crocket Projecting decoration of leaves, flowers or foliage used throughout the Gothic period.

Cusp The projecting points in Gothic tracery.

Dado The section of wall that corresponds to the plinth of a column. The dado moulding or chair rail corresponds to the *cornice* of the plinth, while the skirting is the base.

Damask A reversible fabric patterned by the contrast of raised areas on a plain ground.

Delft ware Tin-glazed earthenware first made at Delft in Holland in the mid-seventeenth century in imitation of oriental porcelain; later copied in England.

Dimity Cotton fabric originally imported from India but later made in Lancashire. The term referred to a number of different types but is now understood to mean a white, slightly ribbed or patterned cotton.

Egg and dart A moulding decorated with a pattern representing alternate eggs and arrow heads.

Entablature The upper part of a classical *order* consisting of, from the top, *cornice*, *frieze* and *architrave*.

Festoon curtain A pull-up curtain that is operated by cords threaded through rings, which can be in a vertical or diagonal line. If the latter the curtain will have 'tails' at each side when pulled up.

Fillet The narrow border that hides the fixing of fabric or paper to walls. It can be plain or decorated, of carved wood, lead, papier maché, or cord.

Frieze The flat centre section of the *entablature*, which can be either plain or decorated. Also the decorated or plain band on a internal wall immediately below the *cornice*.

Fustian Generally a mixture of linen and cotton but sometimes with the addition of wool.

Girandole Candelabra or sconce. Also used as a term for a wall bracket.

Glazing bar (in USA, *muntin*) The member that divides the panes of glass in a window.

Lacquer A very fine hard waterproof surface produced from layers of varnish made from insect secretion or tree sap only to be found in the Far East.

Lambrequin A deeply scalloped piece of drapery.

Marquetry A decorative veneer of naturalistic or figurative forms. See also *parquetry*.

Moreen A worsted fabric with a stamped or watered finish.

Mullion The vertical structural division of a window.

Newel The strong vertical posts in a staircase at corners and at the end of a flight.

Ogee In profile a continuous concave and convex curve – approximately S-shaped.

Order A column consisting of base, shaft, capital and entablature.

Ormolu Bronze gilded by the mercury method.

Parquetry A decorative veneer of geometric forms. See also *marquetry*.

Passementerie Trimmings of braid, fringe, lace and tassels for curtains and upholstery .

Patera Small flat round or oval ornament usually decorated with a stylized flower or foliage.

Pediment The triangular form derived from the gable end above a portico of a classical temple. In interiors used above windows and doors.

Pilaster A pier or shallow rectangular column attached to the wall.

Portière A door curtain.

Quadratura Illusionist architectural painting aimed at extending real architecture into an imaginary space.

Quatrefoil A foil is the curve formed by the projecting cusp of a circle or an arch. The prefix denotes the number of foils.

Rail The horizontal member of the framing of panelling.

Salviata Antonio Salviata (1816–90) produced ornamental and table glass in the Venetian Renaissance style.

Samite A medieval silk embroidered or interwoven with gold.

Sconce A wall light.

Slub To draw out and twist a thread after carding. Slubbed material has a textured surface as the threads are of uneven thickness.

Soffit The underside of the opening of doors, windows, arches, etc.

Solar Upper living-room in a medieval house.

Springing (of an arch) The point at which the curve begins.

Stile The vertical member of the framing of panelling.

Tracery The lace-like intersecting stonework or woodwork in a window or screen.

Transom The horizontal structural division of a window.

Trefoil see *quatrefoil*

Trompe-l'oeil Literally to deceive the eye. Painting which creates the illusion of three dimensions.

Wainscot Timber lining to walls, hence its use as an alternative term for panelling.

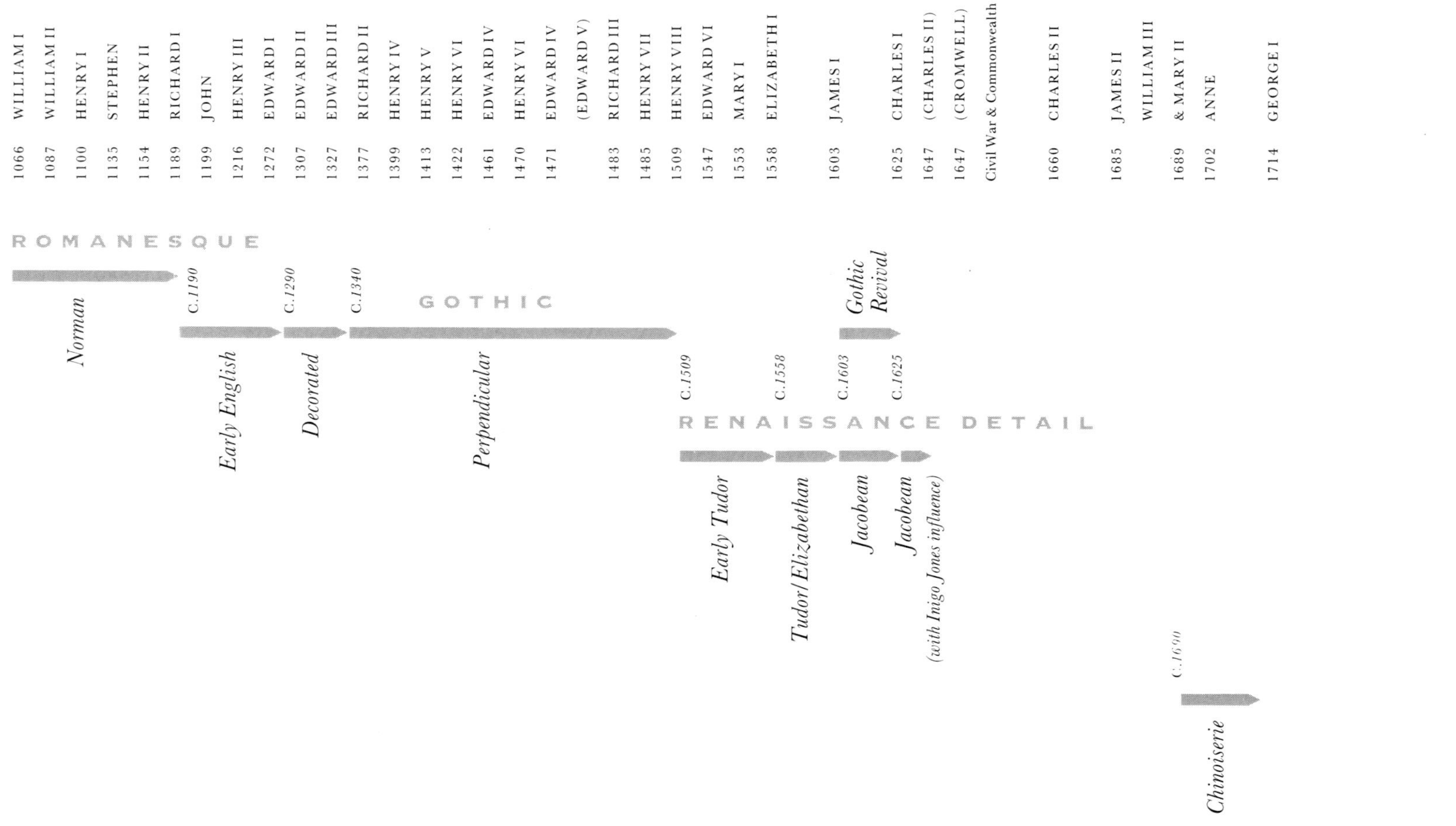
1066 WILLIAM I
1087 WILLIAM II
1100 HENRY I
1135 STEPHEN
1154 HENRY II
1189 RICHARD I
1199 JOHN
1216 HENRY III
1272 EDWARD I
1307 EDWARD II
1327 EDWARD III
1377 RICHARD II
1399 HENRY IV
1413 HENRY V
1422 HENRY VI
1461 EDWARD IV
1470 HENRY VI
1471 EDWARD IV
(EDWARD V)
1483 RICHARD III
1485 HENRY VII
1509 HENRY VIII
1547 EDWARD VI
1553 MARY I
1558 ELIZABETH I
1603 JAMES I
1625 CHARLES I
1647 (CHARLES II)
1647 (CROMWELL)
Civil War & Commonwealth
1660 CHARLES II
1685 JAMES II
WILLIAM III
1689 & MARY II
1702 ANNE
1714 GEORGE I
ROMANESQUE
Norman
C.1190
Early English
C.1290
Decorated
C.1340
GOTHIC
Perpendicular
Gothic Revival
C.1509
C.1558
C.1603
C.1625
RENAISSANCE DETAIL
Early Tudor
Tudor/Elizabethan
Jacobean
Jacobean
(with Inigo Jones influence)
C.1690
Chinoiserie

Chronology

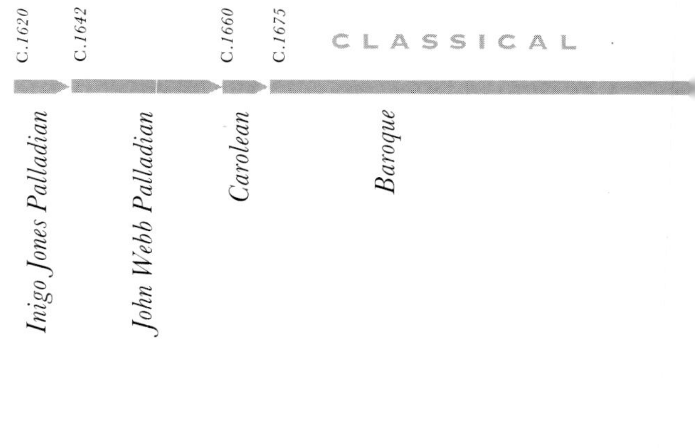
C.1620
C.1642
C.1660
C.1675
CLASSICAL
Inigo Jones Palladian
John Webb Palladian
Carolean
Baroque

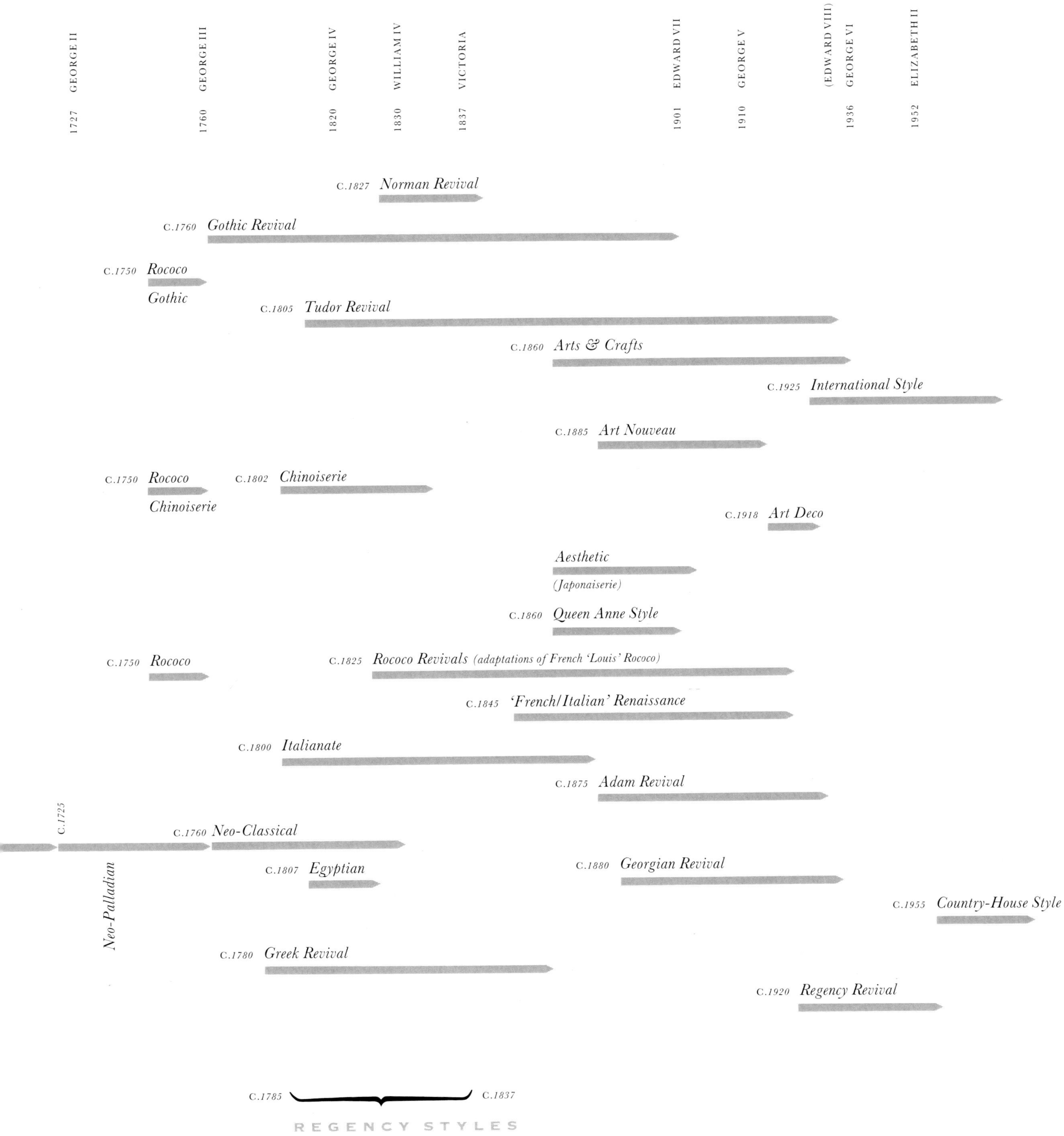
1727 GEORGE II
1760 GEORGE III
1820 GEORGE IV
1830 WILLIAM IV
1837 VICTORIA
1901 EDWARD VII
1910 GEORGE V
(EDWARD VIII)
1936 GEORGE VI
1952 ELIZABETH II
C.1827 Norman Revival
C.1760 Gothic Revival
C.1750 Rococo Gothic
C.1805 Tudor Revival
C.1860 Arts & Crafts
C.1925 International Style
C.1885 Art Nouveau
C.1750 Rococo Chinoiserie
C.1802 Chinoiserie
C.1918 Art Deco
Aesthetic (Japonaiserie)
C.1860 Queen Anne Style
C.1750 Rococo
C.1825 Rococo Revivals (adaptations of French 'Louis' Rococo)
C.1845 'French/Italian' Renaissance
C.1800 Italianate
C.1875 Adam Revival
C.1725
Neo-Palladian
C.1760 Neo-Classical
C.1807 Egyptian
C.1880 Georgian Revival
C.1955 Country-House Style
C.1780 Greek Revival
C.1920 Regency Revival
C.1785
C.1837
REGENCY STYLES

SELECT BIBLIOGRAPHY

ADBURGHAM, ALISON *Shopping in Style, London*, Thames & Hudson, 1979
AGIUS, PAULINE *Ackermann's Regency Furniture and Interiors*, Marlborough, Crowood Press, 1984
ALEXANDER, JONATHAN and BINSKI, PAUL (eds.) *The Age of Chivalry*, catalogue, London, Weidenfeld & Nicolson, 1987
ASLET, CLIVE *The Last Country Houses*, London and New Haven, Yale University Press, 1982
AYRES, JAMES *The Shell Book of the Home in Britain*, London and Boston, Faber & Faber, 1981
BARKER, FELIX N.D. and JACKSON, PETER *London, 2,000 Years of a City and its People*, London, Cassell & Co., 1974
BEARD, GEOFFREY *Craftsmen and Interior Decoration in England 1660-1820*, Edinburgh, John Bartholomew & Son, 1981
BEARD, GEOFFREY *Decorative Plasterwork in Great Britain*, London, Phaidon Press, 1975
BEECHAM, JOHN and anon *The Paper hanger, Painter, Grainer, and Decorator's Assistant*, London, Kent & Co., 1879
BOLD, JOHN, with REEVES, JOHN *Wilton House and English Palladianism*, London, H.M. Stationery Office, 1988
BURTON, ELIZABETH *The Elizabethans at Home*, London, Secker & Warburg, 1963
BYRNE, M. ST. CLARE *The Elizabethan Home*, London, Methuen & Co., 1949
CALLOWAY, STEPHEN *Twentieth-Century Decoration*, London, Weidenfeld & Nicolson, 1988
CHIPPENDALE, THOMAS *The Gentleman and Cabinet-Maker's Director*, (reprint of the third edition), New York, Dover Publications Inc., 1966
CLABBURN, PAMELA *The National Trust Book of Furnishing Textiles*, London, Viking/National Trust, 1988
COLVIN, H.M., RANSOME, D.R. and SUMMERSON, JOHN *The History of the King's Works, Volume III, 1485–1660* (Part I), London, H.M. Stationery Office, 1975
COOKE, EDWARD S. Jr. (ed) *Upholstery in America and Europe from the Seventeenth Century to World War I*, New York, W.W. Norton & Co. Inc., 1987
CORNFORTH, JOHN *English Interiors 1790-1848*, London, Barrie & Jenkins, 1978
CORNFORTH, JOHN *The Inspiration of the Past*, London, Viking/Country Life, 1985
CORNFORTH, JOHN *The Search for a Style*, London, André Deutsch in association with *Country Life*, 1988
CROFT-MURRAY, EDWARD *Decorative Painting in England 1537–1837*, London, Country Life, Vol. 1 1962 Vol. 2 1970
DINKEL, JOHN *The Royal Pavilion, Brighton*, London, Philip Wilson Publishers and Summerfield Press, 1983
EAMES, PENELOPE 'The Power and the Glory', in *Country Life* magazine, London, 31 January, 1985
EASTLAKE, CHARLES L. *Hints on Household Taste, in Furniture, Upholstery and other details*, London, Longmans, Green and Co., 1878

EDIS, ROBERT, W. *Decoration and Furniture of Town Houses*, London, C. Kegan Paul & Co., 1881
EDWARDS, RALPH *The Shorter Dictionary of English Furniture*, London, Country Life, 1964
EVANS, JOAN *Flowering of the Middle Ages*, London, Thames & Hudson, 1966
FAIRFAX-LUCY, ALICE *Mistress of Charlecote*, London, Victor Gollancz, 1987
FERAY, JEAN *Architecture Interieure et Decoration en France des origines à 1875*, Paris, Editions Berger-Levrault – Caisse Nationale des Monuments Historiques et des Sites, 1988
FISHER, RICHARD B. *Syrie Maugham*, London, Gerald Duckworth & Co., 1978
FITZGERALD, BRIAN *Correspondence of Emily, Duchess of Leinster*, Dublin, Dublin Stationery Office, Vol. 1 1949, Vol. 2 1953
FITZ-GERALD, DESMOND *The Norfolk House Music Room*, London, H.M. Stationery Office, 1973
FLEMING, JOHN *Robert Adam and His Circle*, London, John Murray, 1962
FLEMING, JOHN and HONOUR, HUGH *The Penguin Dictionary of Decorative Arts*, London, Penguin Books, 1977
FOWLER, JOHN and CORNFORTH, JOHN *English Decoration in the 18th Century*, London, Barrie & Jenkins, 1974
GERE, CHARLOTTE *Nineteenth-Century Decoration*, London, Weidenfeld & Nicolson, 1989
GIEDION, SIEGFRIED *Mechanization Takes Command*, New York, Oxford University Press, 1948
GILBERT, CHRISTOPHER *The Life and Work of Thomas Chippendale*, London, Cassell, 1978
GILBERT, CHRISTOPHER; LOMAX, JAMES; and WELLS-COLE, ANTHONY *Country House Floors 1660–1850*, Leeds, Leeds City Art Galleries, 1987
GIROUARD, MARK *The Return to Camelot*, London and New Haven, Yale University Press, 1981
GIROUARD, MARK *Sweetness and Light*, Oxford, Oxford University Press, 1977
GIROUARD, MARK *The Victorian Country House*, London, Oxford University Press, 1971
GREGORY, EDWARD W. *The Art and Craft of Homemaking*, London, Thomas Murby & Co., 1925
HALLAM, ELIZABETH *Chronicles of the Age of Chivalry*, London, Guild Publishing, 1987
HALLAM, ELIZABETH *The Plantagenet Chronicles*, London, Guild Publishing, 1986
HARRIS, JOHN and HIGGOTT, GORDON *Inigo Jones, Complete Architectural Drawings*, London, Philip Wilson Publishers for A. Zwemmer, 1989
HARRIS, JOHN; ORGEL, STEPHEN; and STRONG, ROY (eds.) *The King's Arcadia*, London, Arts Council of Great Britain, 1973
HAY, D.R. *The Laws of Harmonious Colouring*, 1844
HICKMAN, PEGGY *A Jane Austen Household Book*, Newton Abbot, David & Charles, 1978
HILL, OLIVER and CORNFORTH, JOHN *English Country Houses – Caroline,*

London, Country Life, 1966
HOBHOUSE, HERMIONE *A History of Regent Street*, London, Macdonald & Jane's, 1975
HOLME, BRYAN *Medieval Pageant*, London, Thames & Hudson, 1987
HONOUR, HUGH *Chinoiserie*, London, John Murray, 1961
HOPE, THOMAS *Household Furniture and Interior Decoration*, New York, Dover Publications, 1971
HUSSEY, CHRISTOPHER *English Country Houses – Early Georgian*, London, Country Life, 1955
HUSSEY, CHRISTOPHER *English Country Houses – Mid Georgian*, London, Country Life, 1956
HUSSEY, CHRISTOPHER *English Country Houses – Late Georgian*, London, Country Life, 1958
HUTH, HANS *Lacquer of the West*, Chicago, University Press of Chicago, 1971
JENKINS, ELIZABETH *Elizabeth the Great*, London, The Companion Book Club, 1958
JOURDAIN, MARGARET *English Decorative Plasterwork of the Renaissance*, London, B.T. Batsford, 1926
JOURDAIN, MARGARET *English Interior Decoration 1500-1830*, London, B.T. Batsford, 1950
JOURDAIN, MARGARET *The Work of William Kent*, London, Country Life, 1948
JORDAN, ROBERT FURNEAUX *Victorian Architecture*, London, Penguin Books, 1966
KIMBALL, FISKE *The Creation of the Rococo Decorative Style*, New York, Dover Publications, 1980
LASDUN, SUSAN *Victorians at Home*, London, Weidenfeld & Nicolson, 1981
LATHAM, ROBERT (ed.) *The Shorter Pepys*, London, Bell & Hyman, 1985
LEES-MILNE, JAMES *English Country Houses – Baroque*, London, Country Life, 1970
LOUDON, J.C. *An Encyclopedia of Cottage, Farm and Villa Architecture and Furniture*, London, 1833
LOWENTHAL, DAVID *The Past is a Foreign Country*, Cambridge, Cambridge University Press, 1985
LLOYD, NATHANIEL *A History of the English House*, London, The Architectural Press, 1931
LYBBE POWYS, MRS PHILIP *Passages from the Diaries of Mrs Lybbe Powys*, edited by Emily J. Climenson, 1899
MINGAY, GORDON *Mrs Hurst Dancing*, London, Victor Gollancz, 1981
MONTGOMERY, FLORENCE M. *Printed Textiles English and American Cottons and Linens 1700-1850*, London, Thames & Hudson, 1970
NAYLOR, GILLIAN *The Arts and Crafts Movement*, London, Studio Vista, 1971
OMAN, CHARLES C. and HAMILTON JEAN *Wallpapers. A History and Catalogue of the Collection in the Victoria and Albert Museum*, London, Philip Wilson Publishers for Sotheby Publications, 1982
O'NEILL, DANIEL *Lutyens Country Houses*, London, Lund Humphries Publishers, 1980
PUCKLER-MUSKAU, Prince Hermann, *A Regency Visitor*, London, Collins, 1957
RIDLEY, JASPER *The Tudor Age*, London, Constable, 1988
RILEY, H.T. *Memorials of London and London Life in the Thirteenth, Fourteenth and Fifteenth Centuries*, 1868
ROBERTS, JANE *Hans Holbein the Younger*, London, Oresko Books, 1979
ROBINSON, STUART *A History of Printed Textiles*, London, Studio Vista, 1969
LA ROCHE, SOPHIE VON *Sophie in London, 1786*, London, Jonathan Cape, 1933
SAINT, ANDREW *Richard Norman Shaw*, London and New Haven, Yale University Press, 1976
SCHOESER, MARY and RUFFEY, CELIA *English and American Textiles from 1790 to the Present*, London, Thames & Hudson, 1989
SERVICE, ALISTAIR *Edwardian Interiors*, London, Barrie & Jenkins, 1982
SHERATON, THOMAS *The Cabinet-Maker and Upholsterer's Drawing-Book*, New York, Dover Publications, 1972
SIMPSON, DUNCAN *C.F.A. Voysey*, London, Lund Humphries Publishers, 1979
SNODIN, MICHAEL (ed.) *Rococo*, catalogue, London, Victoria and Albert Museum in association with Trefoil Books, 1984
STILLMAN, DAMIE *English Neo-Classical Architecture*, London, A. Zwemmer, 1988
SUMMERSON, JOHN *Architecture in Britain 1530-1830*, London, Penguin Books, 1979
SYKES, CHRISTOPHER SIMON *Private Palaces*, London, Chatto & Windus, 1985
SYMONDS, R.W. and WHINERAY B.B. *Victorian Furniture*, London, Studio Editions, 1987
THOMPSON, PAUL *The Work of William Morris*, London, Heinemann, 1967
THOMSON, F.P. *Tapestry, Mirror of History*, Newton Abbot, David & Charles, 1980
THOMSON, W.G. *A History of Tapestry*, London, E.P. Publishing Co., 1973
THORNTON, PETER *Authentic Decor*, London, Weidenfeld & Nicolson, 1984
THORNTON, PETER *Baroque and Rococo Silks*, New York, Taplinger Publishing Co., 1965
THORNTON, PETER *Seventeenth-Century Interior Decoration in England, France and Holland*, New Haven and London, Yale University Press, 1978
THORNTON, P.K. and TOMLIN, M.F. *The Furnishing and Decoration of Ham House*, London, The Furniture History Society, 1980
TOMLIN, MAURICE *Ham House*, London, Victoria and Albert Museum, 1986
TOMLIN, MAURICE and HARDY, JOHN *Osterley Park House*, London, Victoria and Albert Museum, 1985
TURNER, MARK and others *Art Nouveau Designs from the Silver Studio Collections*, London, Middlesex Polytechnic, 1986
TURNER, T.H. and PARKER, J.H. *Some account of domestic architecture in England from the Conquest to Henry VIII*, Oxford, 1851–9
WAINWRIGHT, CLIVE *The Romantic Interior*, New Haven and London, Yale University Press, 1989
WAINWRIGHT, CLIVE and others *George Bullock*, London, John Murray, 1988
WELLS-COLE, ANTHONY *Historic Paper Hangings from Temple Newsam and other English Houses*, Leeds, Leeds City Art Galleries, 1983
WHATMAN, SUSANNA *The Housekeeping Book of Susanna Whatman*, London, Century Hutchinson, 1987
WINCHESTER, BARBARA *Tudor Family Portrait*, London, Jonathan Cape, 1955
WINGFIELD DIGBY, GEORGE *The Devonshire Hunting Tapestries*, London, H.M. Stationery Office, 1971
WITTKOWER, RUDOLF *Palladio and English Palladianism*, New York, Thames & Hudson, 1983
WOOD, MARGARET *The English Mediaeval House*, New York, Harper & Row, 1983

* *

The Buildings of England edited by Nikolaus Pevsner & others, Penguin Books
Country Life magazine, from 1897
National Trust guidebooks
National Trust yearbooks and studies 1975–81
Ministry of Works and Department of the Environment guidebooks

HOUSES AND THEIR LOCATIONS

*Denotes house open to the public, either on a regular basis or by request. Houses and castles no longer in existence are not listed.

ABBOTSFORD,* Melrose, Scotland
THE ADELPHI, London
A LA RONDE,* Exmouth, Devon
ASHCOMBE TOWER, Ashcombe, South Devon
ATTINGHAM PARK,* nr. Shrewsbury, Shropshire
BANQUETING HOUSE,* Whitehall, London
BEDE HOUSE,* Lyddington, Leicestershire
BELTON HOUSE,* nr. Grantham, Lincolnshire
BENTLEYS (BENTLEY WOOD),* Halland, East Sussex
BLENHEIM PALACE,* Woodstock, Oxfordshire
BOLSOVER CASTLE,* Derbyshire
BRADLEY MANOR,* Newton Abbot, Devon
BRANTWOOD,* Coniston, Cumbria
BRODSWORTH HALL, nr. Doncaster, South Yorkshire
CANONS ASHBY HOUSE,* Canons Ashby, Northamptonshire
CARDIFF CASTLE,* Cardiff, South Glamorgan, Wales
CASTEL COCH,* Tongwynlais, South Glamorgan
CASTLE ASHBY, nr. Northampton, Northamptonshire
CASTLE HEDINGHAM, nr. Halstead, Essex
CASTLE HOWARD,* nr. York, North Yorkshire
CHARLECOTE PARK,* nr. Stratford-upon-Avon, Warwickshire
CHASTLETON HOUSE,* nr. Moreton-in-Marsh, Oxfordshire
CHATSWORTH,* Bakewell, Derbyshire
CHISWICK HOUSE,* Chiswick, London
CLANDON PARK,* nr. Guildford, Surrey
CLAYDON HOUSE,* Middle Claydon, nr. Winslow, Buckinghamshire
CLIVEDEN (now an hotel),* nr. Maidenhead, Berkshire
CRAGSIDE HOUSE,* Rothbury, Northumberland
THE DEANERY, Sonning, Berkshire
THE DEEPDENE, Dorking, Surrey
DITCHLEY PARK,* nr. Charlbury, Oxfordshire
DRAYTON HOUSE,* Lowick, Kettering, Northumberland
DYRHAM PARK,* nr. Bath, Avon
EASTNOR CASTLE,* nr. Ledbury, Hereford and Worcester
ELTHAM LODGE (Golf Club), Eltham, Kent
FARNBOROUGH HALL,* nr. Banbury, Warwickshire
FELBRIGG HALL,* nr. Cromer, Norfolk
GAWTHORPE HALL,* Padiham, Lancashire
GROVELANDS, Southgate, London
HADDON HALL,* Bakewell, Derbyshire
HAM HOUSE,* Richmond, London
HARDWICK HALL,* nr. Chesterfield, Derbyshire
HAREWOOD HOUSE,* nr. Leeds, West Yorkshire
HEVENINGHAM, nr. Halesworth, Suffolk
HILL COURT, Ross on Wye, Hereford and Worcester
HILL HALL, Theydon Mount, Essex
HOLKHAM HALL,* Wells, Norfolk
HOUGHTON HALL,* Kings Lynn, Norfolk
KEDLESTON HALL,* Derby, Derbyshire
KELMARSH, nr. Market Harborough, Northamptonshire
KELMSCOTT MANOR,* Kelmscott, Oxfordshire
KENSINGTON PALACE,* Kensington, London
KENWOOD,* Hampstead, London
KNOLE,* Sevenoaks, Kent
LANCASTER HOUSE, St. James's, London
LONGTHORPE TOWER,* Peterborough, Cambridgeshire
LOSELEY HOUSE,* Guildford, Surrey
MAWLEY HALL,* Cleobury Mortimer, Shropshire
NARFORD, Narborough, Norfolk
NOSTELL PRIORY,* Wakefield, West Yorkshire
OAKWELL HALL,* Birstall, West Yorkshire
OSBORNE HOUSE,* Cowes, Isle of Wight
OSTERLEY PARK HOUSE,* Osterley, London
OWLPEN MANOR, nr. Dursley, Gloucestershire
OXBURGH HALL,* Swaffham, Norfolk
PENCARROW HOUSE,* Bodmin, Cornwall
PENRHYN CASTLE,* Bangor, Gwynedd, Wales
PETWORTH HOUSE,* Petworth, West Sussex
PORT LYMPNE,* Lympne, Hythe, Kent
QUEEN'S HOUSE,* Greenwich, London
RED HOUSE,* Red Lane, Bexleyheath, London
ROYAL PAVILION,* Brighton, East Sussex
RUFFORD OLD HALL,* Rufford, nr. Ormskirk, Lancashire
ST. JAMES'S PALACE, St. James's, London
SALTRAM HOUSE,* Plymouth, Devon
SCARISBRICK, Southport, Lancashire
SHELTON OAK PRIORY, Shrewsbury, Shropshire
SIR JOHN CASS SCHOOL, London
SOUTHILL, nr. Biggleswade, Bedfordshire
SIZERGH CASTLE,* Kendal, Cumbria
STRAWBERY HILL, Twickenham, London
SUDBURY HALL,* nr. Derby, Derbyshire
SYON HOUSE,* Brentford, London
TEMPLE NEWSAM,* Leeds, West Yorkshire
VICTORIA AND ALBERT MUSEUM,* South Kensington, London
THE VYNE,* Basingstoke, Hampshire
WENTWORTH CASTLE (Adult Education College), nr. Barnsley, West Yorkshire
WESTMINSTER HALL, Westminster, London
WILTON HOUSE,* Wilton, Wiltshire
WOODHALL PARK (Heath Mount School),* Watton-at-Stone, Hertfordshire

INDEX

Figures in *italics* indicate illustration numbers